I HUNG MY HARP ON THE WILLOW TREE

by Andrew Fralick

I HUNG MY HARP ON THE WILLOW TREE

ISBN: 9781080638499

www.drewfralick.com
@realdrewfralick

Cover Design and Illustration by Grayson Stallings
www.graysonstallings.com

Dedicated to all the comics and generous laughers in Shanghai. It doesn't matter if the joke is funny, as long as they know it's over.

The Elevator Pitch for This Book

Somebody once told me that I should prepare an elevator pitch. That's where you're riding in an elevator with, let's say, the CEO of Goldman Sachs or Costco or something and he's going up to the 57th floor, but you're going to the 12th floor because you're just delivering Chinese carry-out and those guys on the 57th floor have their own private buffet, so they obviously don't eat General Tzo's chicken combination platter for lunch (Obviously!), and the CEO turns around and says something like "Hey, what's your deal?" And you say something so clever and concise about yourself that by the time the elevator dings at the 12th floor he has made you a VP in his company.

This book began as a lengthy farewell letter to my friends in Shanghai. I lived in China for over ten years and during that time went from being an English teacher, to quality control guy in a factory, to eventually becoming a mental health counselor and stand up comedian. By the end, I was working at a psychiatric hospital during the day and the comedy club at night, and sometimes the line between the two got blurry.

My friends and I were at ground zero when comedy started to become a thing in China. We went on tour to places most people couldn't even pronounce (Wuxi, Hangzhou, Hefei) and shared life and conversation over coffee, beer, shishas, and in late night dining spots. I believe there is nothing sweeter in comedy than to be known. Each time we go on stage with the hope of being known. This book was my effort to be known on a deeper level by my friends, and now by you, dear reader.

I saw many talented people start doing comedy, steadily grow over the course of several years but then hit a plateau for no apparent reason. Likewise, there have been long stretches for me in which I didn't enjoy getting up and each show felt like a chore. During those times, my confidence was super low and I had no faith in any joke. When you think you have 30 minutes of material only to discover you have 3, it can be so disheartening. In those times I found it helpful to answer the question 'Why?' Why am I doing this? What am I trying to say about me? What am I saying about the world we live in? If you can answer *why* then you can keep going. Or you can stop. You can decide there's another, better path for you. When you open yourself up to *why*, many creative possibilities become available.

Comics have a special calling in life. We are the auditors of narrative, called in by society to closely examine the authenticity of a story when things get out of hand. Comics are able to bring healing by gaining mastery over painful experiences. There is also access to the joy of making people laugh while not necessarily having to go deep or dark.

All that being said, here's my elevator pitch: This book is about comedy (ding), mental health (ding), my own time in China (ding), and finally the narrative I've tried to build my life around (ding). If anything in here is helpful, feel free to use it. If halfway through the book you throw up your hands and declare what I've written malarkey, the book can also be used to prop up the corner of your pool table that's starting to sag.

A.F.
1 December 2018

The
Art
of LOL

ONE

Signal and Noise

Comedy is a fragile art form. A show can be completely undone by even the smallest of distractions. Poor lighting, noise bleed, loud bartenders, even someone in the audience laughing too hard can make an expertly crafted joke or message come undone; and if one of these can kill the magic of comedy, then how much more a large distraction?

One time I hosted a show at a steakhouse with an all-you-can-eat buffet running down the middle of the room. As a side note, all-you-can-eat buffets and comedy are incompatible: if the food is good, the comedy will be terrible (no laughter). If the comedy is good, then it's a severe choking hazard. And as everybody in the business knows, rule number one is safety first.

On this particular night a group of guys was asked to leave because they hadn't paid for the meal. As the show began and people got settled in with their chicken fried steak, mashed potatoes and canned green beans, the promoter and these guys began shouting loudly at each other from the back of the room. The promoter had to kick them out. Boy was it awkward!

As the host of the show, I tried to control the situation: asking the gentleman seated in the front row where he was from, was the woman seated next to him his sister (obviously it was his wife), etcetera. But no one was paying attention to my genius crowd work. Instead, all eyes were on them as they walked from the back of the restaurant to the door and left.

The backdrop to the stage was a large window that looked out onto the street, and you could see the guys starting to shove the promoter and taunting him to fight. How could you expect anyone to listen to my jokes when a live reenactment of Rocky 5 was happening right behind the stage? (That's the one where Stallone is all old and blown out and street fights the teenager. Not the one where he beats the Russian.)

Now if rather than comedy I were in a death metal band or were a DJ, do you think this fight would distract from the show? No way! It would make the show even 5 times better. Hence, mosh pits. Indeed, comedy is a fragile art form and I've seen far less than this throw the show off. However, audiences recognize and respect the vulnerability of comedy.

I recently watched a DVD of a John Mayer concert. In between sets he was talking to the audience, sharing some of his thoughts on life and telling a few jokes. But he's got a guitar, he's not vulnerable. Nobody wants to hear your musings on life John, just play *Daughters* man, that's why we came. By contrast, I am delighted to listen to Dave Chapelle's thoughts on any topic. An audience senses the vulnerability and this weakness gives comedy its strength. It is stripped down and bare, nothing but a space, a voice, a soul amongst souls. Simply put it is art and the comic is the canvas.

Performance perception: signal to noise ratio
Standup comedy, unlike other forms of entertainment (e.g. hockey) has no objective scoring mechanism. Therefore the only way to really say whether some comedy was 'good' or 'not good' is by going off of an audience's perception. However, most audiences remain unaware of what goes into their perception of a performance. An experienced comic will recognize the dynamics being played out during a show, with not only the performers on stage, but also the audience and the

venue. Comics say things to each other backstage like, "ugh, it's not an easy room", but don't always clarify what specifically is making it a hard room. Comics work actively to improve those areas that make a performance good, but generally spend less time decreasing those factors that make a performance bad.

Given the vulnerability of standup, one of the main factors that can dramatically lower the perception of a performance is a poorly run room, whereas a well run room will diminish distractions and make comics look their best. How the fragility of this art form is protected marks a major distinction between a 'comedy room' or 'a room where comedy is done' (e.g. bar shows, a show at the local VFW or shows in a rented mop closet). Understanding the different elements factoring into a show is useful for understanding how a performance will be perceived. A concept than can be utilized to examine this is 'signal to noise ratio' (S/N ratio) which is used regularly in manufacturing and engineering. The original S/N ratio looked like this[1]:

$$\eta = \frac{Signal}{noise} = 10\frac{l}{r}\left[\frac{S_\beta - V_e}{V_N}\right]$$

To apply (and vastly simplify) this formula for use in comedy, let us say the following:

$$perception\ of\ performance = \frac{signal: a\ number\ from\ 0 - 10}{noise: a\ number\ from\ 1 - 10}$$

Signal are the parts of the show that are adding to the pleasure of experiencing a show, whereas noise are aspects that detract from that experience. Think of a show as scotch whiskey. There's a lot that goes into the process of making scotch, but in the end a customer just wants those good or pure parts to drink. That's signal. Whereas noise is all the toxins that don't get filtered out of a cheaply made whiskey and end up giving one a headache the next day.

signal= sum of all factors which add to the show (rated from 0-10, 10 being the best)
<u>examples of signal:</u>
- good lighting
- quality sound system
- attentive and excited audience
- high performance ability
- well written material

noise = sum of all factors distracting or detracting from the show (rated from 1-10, 1= no noise)
<u>examples of noise:</u>
- poor or no lighting (e.g. room is too bright)
- microphone cuts in and out
- audience is there for another event (besides comedy)
- performer is poorly prepared or inexperienced
- actual noise (e.g. television is on in the background at a bar show)

By this equation a numerical rating can be given to a room or show. Notice that the signal is divided by the noise, not subtracted. This is an important distinction. An expert comic can gain back some of the potential to get laughs, but his effort or skill do not outright cancel the effects of noise in a show.

First, take as an example a 3 year comic with strong material and below average performance ability. This comic is producing a moderate signal strength. The venue in this scenario is a black box theatre, with a good sound system, a room which is ¾ full and the audience is enjoying themselves. Therefore the noise level is quite low. Let us assume the following:

3 YEAR COMIC @ Black Box Theatre:
(moderate signal strength) **6** */ (low noise level)* **1.5 = 4.0**

A total score of 4. In other words, this comic won't kill but he'll walk away from the gig having made a good impression on the audience. However if you take a high level pro, i.e. Mr. Pro Comic, who has 25 years of experience, (very strong material plus excellent performance ability) and put him in that same room, he will look like a genius:

MR. PRO COMIC @ Black Box Theatre:
(strong signal strength) **9.5** */ (low noise level*)* **1.5 = 6.333**

*(A noise level of 1.0 while theoretically possible is literally impossible)

But let's say that Mr. Pro Comic isn't booked on any gigs that night, so instead he decides to hop on an open mic at the local mexican restaurant, Los Amigos Dos. At this show, the cook keeps walking in front of the stage to carry trash bags to the dumpster outside, the audience is distracted or drunk and the microphone keeps cutting in and out. This is a room with a high noise level. Let us assume a noise factor of 3.5:

MR. PRO COMIC @ Los Amigos Dos Open Mic:
(strong signal strength) **9.5** */ (high noise level)* **3.5 = 2.71**

This score of 2.71 of course leaves our enchilada filled patrons who have seen Mr. Pro Comic on TV muttering to themselves, "geez, that guy was a lot funnier on Fallon", all the while not realizing that the magic of comedy can only happen in a somewhat protected environment. This is why when your uncle finds out that you've been doing comedy and at Thanksgiving dinner says in front of everyone "Come on! Tell us a joke!" you should slap him on the top of his bald ugly head.

Now let's say the next day, two friends, one who was at the black box theatre show and one who was at the Mexican restaurant gig, meet up for coffee. Mexican restaurant lady says to her friend, "I saw Mr. Pro Comic at the Los Amigos 2 open mic last night and he was *not* funny!" Black box theatre girl remarks how odd, she was also at a comedy show last night! At her show there was this new guy who was kinda awkward (below average performance ability) but also super funny (strong material). This may lead the two friends to the conclusion that 3 Year Comic is possibly a more skilled and talented comedian than Mr. Pro Comic. Though there are equations in these examples, this is not actual science. However if you're reading this and trying to decide on a topic for your doctoral dissertation, you're welcome.

Keep in mind that some rooms are so bad and some distractions so huge that it takes an elite level comic to have a good set. Moreover, some noise is too much for anyone to be successful. Extremely high-level noise scenarios (like an open mic at a sports bar whilst the Detroit Lions are on the verge of winning their first playoff game since Bill Clinton was considered a family man) will end the show no matter who is on stage.

Some of the most impressive performances I've ever seen were in high noise conditions. Once on a late night showcase I saw an intoxicated audience member collapse while leaving during the host's opening set. It was such a nasty fall that I thought the guy had died. Of course, in most situations the show would have ended abruptly. To everyone's surprise the host just continued his set. "The show must go on," he said. As everyone waited for the ambulance to arrive and while the paramedics were treating the guy in the back of the room, the host performed what I can only describe as the most inspired 45 minutes of comedy I have ever seen. He made fun of the guy laying on the ground, roasted him even, but also reassured the dude's friends and kept everyone laughing. I don't know how it's possible but he made what was happening okay, he turned noise into signal.

That is one mark of a great comic, the ability to turn noise into signal. That is why people respond so strongly to the takedown of a heckler. When a heckler pounces, the noise level shoots up, but when a comic turns it into signal the show just gets better and better.

Algorithm for a Hacky Joke

How are we to understand the difference between a joke that is 'hacky' and a joke that's not? Hacky seems to imply a cheapness, a lack of something. Is it a lack of creativity? Lack of performance ability? Lack of depth? Often it seems that hacky material is performed with a well-polished delivery, hence the commonly heard statement, "His material gets huge laughs, but it is so hacky." Hack is a kind of blunt force trauma. A surgeon makes an incision, only cutting what is absolutely necessary, but a medieval knight hacks off the arm of his rival. You use a hacksaw to chop down a tree, not to make furniture. Though hack may be immediately gratifying and spectacular to watch, it leaves the audience with no memory, whereas to say someone's comedy is incisive means it gets down to the heart of the matter.

That's why I wonder whether hackiness also points towards a lack of emotional authenticity. In both the counseling room and the comedy club there are two kinds of truth: factual and emotional. Most areas of life are concerned with the factual truths of a situation, but comedy aims for emotional truth. This is what makes a comic potentially powerful.

***

That being said, here's how to write a hacky joke:

To drive home the point that you are really local, use the following algorithm to create jokes for the audiences' listening pleasure:

"Hello! I'm from [insert place], which if you've never heard of it, it's the [insert crappy place] of [insert place near where the gig is]."

When introducing where you're from remember to use the phrase "…or as I like to call it …". If you're ever in a bind, just use Cleveland, Ohio as a reference. Then at the end of this Cleveland based statement add the phrase "Or as I like to call it, THE MISTAKE BY THE LAKE!!" You want to be sure to enunciate the words THE. MIS. TAKE. BY. THE. LAKE., say them loudly and slowly. If you are wearing a tie on stage, be sure to sort of grab your tie and twist it as you say these words.

And also act like it's the funniest and most clever thing you've ever said, rather than a line you've been saying every night for the last twenty five years at the small club in Milwaukee that you're a regular at. Of course it's not just places this algorithm works for, you can insert just about anything:

[a] is the [b] of [c]

For example, here is an outline for a joke:

_____ is the Walmart of _____.

This joke becomes the centerpiece of your act when it's expanded to include hilarious and clever examples. As in the case of:

_____ is the Walmart of _____.
Example 1.
Example 2.
Example 3 that is both clever and hilarious.

Cleveland is the Walmart of Ohio
Everybody there is fat
You'll feel normal walking around in camo
And there's lots of people living out of their cars in the parking lot!

By this point the audience will be madly laughing. The applause breaks will be crashing in wave upon wave, but if you find an opening, take advantage of the good thing you've got going on stage by screaming one more time "IT'S THE MISTAKE BY THE LAKE PEOPLE!!" for good measure. Then drop the mic and walk triumphantly off stage. Also, when you get a job as a writer on the John Oliver show, don't forget those of us who knew you before you were successful.

***

Going back to the idea of emotional truth versus factual truth, we can say that comedy tends to appeal to the former. Some of the most wildly inaccurate and offensive things have been said on the comedy stage, but at the end of the day the only real sin in comedy is to not be funny or entertaining. I've seen people make great points during a laughter-free set, that's called a Ted Talk, not a joke. People come to a comedy club to laugh, if they wanted information they would have audited a class at the local community college.

I am by no stretch of the imagination a comedy purist. I believe there is no right or wrong way to do comedy. The stories of Andy Kaufmann, whose concept of a laugh spilled off the stage, into the street and out into life are deeply inspiring. Alternatively, Netflix is filled with the specials of straight comics who would never dream of bringing even a glass of water on stage with them, and their material never dips beyond airplane food and relationships. I've seen men in chicken suits do a cover of the *The Lumineers* that I laughed at til I cried, and I've also stood in the back of the room as my opener covered Melissa Etheridge and rolled my eyes in disgust. There is no right or wrong way to do it. If someone gets to the point that they're selling out Madison Square Garden and not saying anything at all, and they're the comedy equivalent of Pitbull, there is a kind of low-brow appeal to that as well. If they are happy and making a living, or unhappy, or whatever, I do not judge.

All I'm saying is that the potential for expressing emotional truth is there. There is a possibility of connecting with people in a deep way. Deep down most comics want to be known and accepted in their most intimate parts (just like everybody else). Psychologically speaking, that is why there are so many dick jokes.

Carl Rogers, a pioneer in the counseling field, said that genuine connection with a client was necessary and sufficient to affect change in another's life. Numerous studies have also attested to the fact that the largest determinant of whether psychotherapy will be successful or not is the bond formed between counselor and client. Perhaps the same is also true for a comic and the audience.

References:

1. Christensen, Eldon H. *The certified quality process analyst handbook* (2007) American Society for Quality, Quality Press, Milwaukee, USA, pg. 94

TWO
Psychotherapy and Comedy As Mirroring Art Forms

The road to genuine connection with an audience happens on a macro-level over the course of a career and on a micro-level over the course of a one hour set. This connection grows in three distinct stages that are also seen in the standard one hour timeframe of a counseling session.

Psychotherapy and stand-up comedy are art forms that mirror each other in almost every way. Counseling being the dark Yin to Comedy's Yang. Counseling is the art of receiving, listening, reflecting. A posture of stillness and anonymity. Comedy however is a naked projection out into an audience which is unseen, shrouded in darkness.

They say that comedic timing is one of the most difficult skills to learn, it is pure instinct. For counselors, timing is also a skill that textbooks are unable to teach. Therapists sit with a client and listen, wait, ask questions, and listen more, all the while waiting for that moment when a well placed hunch, insight or question could be therapeutic.

Is it a coincidence that one therapy session is about an hour and headlining a comedy show is about an hour? Not only are they approximately the same length, I see them as having a similar structure. One book that I have found helpful for understanding the structure of a therapy session is *The Clinical Interview Using DSM-IV-TR Volume 1* by Othmer and Othmer[1].

I believe comics can read this book to gain some inspiration when writing an hour long set. In this book it talks about the three stages of an hour session: *opening*, *middle*, and *ending* phases. Main tasks of these stages are outlined below.

Table 1.
Three stages of counseling and comedy

Phase/Stage	Counseling*	Comedy
OPENING PHASE (STAGE 1)	Interviewer warms up the patient, establishes rapport, and prepares the patient for the main task of the interview.	Comic builds trust, proves credibility, establishes rapport, and tells jokes. **"I can be funny"**
MIDDLE PHASE (STAGE 2)	Interviewer performs the bulk of the work, therefore this phase takes the longest time.	Comic deepens rapport, uses storytelling, and relates life story. **"Who I am"**
CLOSING PHASE (STAGE 3)	Interviewer prepares the patient for closure. Therapist avoids highly emotional topics, summarizes for the patient what has been learned and provides an outlook for the future.	Relating of one's life philosophy -Gaining mastery over trauma -Disarming violence and oppression **"What I think"**
*source: Othmer and Othmer		

Stage 1

In a therapy hour, the opening stage is extremely important. Research has shown that the most important element for the success of therapy is the quality of the relationship shared between client and counselor. Not only is it important for clients to like their counselor, it is also crucial that there be a sense of the counselor's expertise, in other words a belief that the counselor is able to do what they say they can do. Successes early on in the counseling process can reinforce the belief that the counselor knows what they're talking about and pushes the momentum of therapy forward.

In the same way, a comic must prove to an audience that they have expertise as well, that they are able to make an audience laugh. In my experience audiences generally decide whether or not a comic has this ability in about 10 seconds to 2 minutes, unless they know the comic (e.g. a celebrity, or have previously seen the comic perform).

The opening stage of a therapy hour is about building rapport. An important component of building rapport is convincing your clients that you have the expertise to address their concerns. This could be done in several ways including giving empathic statements, listening intently, or displaying expert knowledge about a psychiatric issue. Beyond that, a client also makes judgements about the expertise of their therapist simply based on appearance and posture. People don't want to see a therapist who looks young or well rested. They want an old, poorly dressed, professorly type, with a gray beard who looks like he moonlights as the mascot for a fish sticks company. One more thing, if the therapist has a pipe and many old books in their office I've heard that's helpful as well.

Stage 1 in comedy, much like in therapy, is about reading the room (empathy) and reassuring the audience that you can make them laugh (display of expert knowledge). For an hour long set, this stage can take anywhere from 10 to 35 minutes. Many performers will not leave this stage for the entirety of the hour. However, if a comic never leaves Stage 1 material, the audience may walk away from the show entertained but have no real sense of who the comic is as a person. Often heavily intoxicated crowds or shows performed under special circumstances (e.g. corporate gigs) will not lend themselves to venturing past Stage 1 material. There is absolutely nothing wrong with this. Almost nobody has the luxury of performing 30 minute sets or longer every night. So comics operate mostly in the realm of Stage 1.

Stage 2

Stage 2 material is more about who a comic is, that is, their personal narrative. The first third of an hour is about hitting as many punchlines as possible, whereas the second third of a set transitions into storytelling, with laughs spaced further apart. This "one third of an hour principal" applies to sitcoms, which are also about twenty to twenty-five minutes long. That is the approximate amount of time people can be entertained before they are ready to transition to the next thing. Entry into Stage 2 switches performance gears, allowing a reset to the audience and enabling the lengthening of attention. Live performances, movies, books and music also operate by the same concept. If a comic has done well in the first twenty minutes, the audience will have laughed heartily and that initial burst of energy has been burned through. The show will require variation to keep people going.

With genuine empathy comes a natural curiosity about who the performer is. Personal narrative is appropriate for this middle section of an hour, where the audience can gain insight into the performer's line of thinking. Relating of experiences also increases the connection with audience members as they find commonalities with what is being talked about. This builds trust between comic and crowd, and trust is a necessary factor for wading into the depths of Stage 3 comedy.

Stage 3

In the closing phase a message is delivered. This is what could be called a life philosophy. It's beyond the middle phase where one introduces who they are. The comic has related their story and now the audience can hear what that story has led them to believe.

Stage 3 material is extremely difficult to write, practice and is not palatable for many audience members or even fans. If Stage 3 material is performed on an open mic or a 15 minute slot opening for someone else, it's 95% guaranteed to bomb. One time I opened for a headlining comic with a 12-minute long bit about people's indifference to human trafficking and it was one of the worst comedic decisions I have ever made. Indeed, some people come to shows just to laugh and don't want anything that is deeper or thought provoking. Some would disagree that this closing phase is even important. However, those who write and perform into this phase go beyond entertainment and into the realm of impact.

***

I saw a guy at the gym one time wearing a shirt that said 'Pain is fear leaving the body'. Comedy has its own mantra:'Laughter is pain leaving the mind'. That's because humor is considered a high level coping mechanism. Most jokes involve discomfort or pain. I've never seen a comic do a joke (unironically) about how well they were getting along with their spouse. The pain content of jokes ranges on a spectrum from the annoyance of flying economy class to the fear of death itself. Some material, like memories, is 'too soon': not enough time has passed from the incident to the point where people are able to laugh about what happened. Some people are too far removed from a trauma to legitimately make a joke out of it. For instance, an audience will often accept a victim making a joke of their own pain, whereas those perceived to have helped the perpetrator or to have never experienced that form of victimization will be met with stony silence. "What would you know about [fill in the blank]?" the audience may think. A comic is always allowed to joke about their own pain though and some have hypothesized that those with a lot of unprocessed pain are drawn to stand up.

The deeper a comic climbs into a painful moment the harder it gets to keep an audience engaged. However, if done well it will leave them with a lasting impression and a changed view of the world. In counseling, treatment is considered a success when the client casts aside their self-defeating beliefs in favor of beliefs that help them become more fulfilled. Sometimes an indicator that a trauma has lost its grip on a person is they are able to laugh about the event. This is not to say the person completely stops hurting, but that the pain has lost a certain potency.

The holy grail of stand up is to relate, process, and get a laugh from a traumatic memory. This material is normally not present in stage 1 or even in stage 2. Stage 1 material is what makes one good at comedy, stage 2 is what builds an audience. Stage 3 is something else entirely. This concept is a central theme of the book *A Horse Walks into a Bar* by David

Grossman. In the book the main character Dov, a veteran comic, keeps pushing his audience to Stage 3, but they desperately resist so he is required to insert Stage 1 material to keep them fed for the journey to his dark place. To talk about something that hurts so badly, to have a live audience relate with that dark place and in the end everyone can laugh about it is a deeply cathartic experience for everyone involved.

References:

1. Othmer E., Othmer S.C. *The Clinical Interview Using DSM IV TR, Vol. 1: Fundamentals* (2001) American Psychiatric Publishing

THREE

THE ART OF LOL

Table 2. Humorous Phenomenons
1. Large fruit being thrown off a building
2. Animals in outfits
3. Off-key children's choirs

Musicality of a joke

Comics with a writing block should visit the local zoo. Hopefully they won't go alone, because from an outsider perspective that seems so miserable. (Is there anything sadder than a solitary, fully grown man eating an overpriced hotdog and peering into the camel pen at noon on a workday?) Zoos can be a source of inspiration because animals are wildly pleasing and funny in their movements. Think about it, how funny is a donkey in captivity or a flock of geese at feeding time? Children love watching a walrus play with a ball or a goat chewing on grass. I even saw a man throw Pringles at a baboon.

Writer's block indicates that life is too heavy. Getting in touch with one's inner child involves shedding fear and shame, but somewhere deep down inside, that little kid is still there. The ability to delight in nature and animals is inherent in humans and can help take jokes that have gone stale and give them a fresh energy.

The sound of nature is singing. All plants and animals sing in their own way, and that sound is pleasing to the soul. In modern life, especially urban life, days or weeks can go by without hearing these songs; whereas in the past, life was closely integrated into nature. Comedy tends to shy away from nature as it is distracting and chaotic. Some of the worst shows I've ever seen were held outdoors. Comedy prefers darkness and blackout, rather than the greens and yellows of nature, or the cawing and barking of animals. Yet this singing of nature still appeals to the soul deep down. The purity of nature draws one in.

Take the elephant for example. Go find me a five-year-old who doesn't love elephants. They have big feet, long funny looking snouts, and cute little eyes (elephants). Looking at an elephant, it's hard to know what's going through its mind, but clearly there's an innocence. Elephants don't have neurotic thoughts. They're not out there humbly bragging on Facebook about how "blessed they are to have such delicious peanuts, #grateful". They just are what they are. Some of that genuineness seen in animals can be cultivated by connecting regularly with nature. Comedy audiences find that genuineness hard to define, but will know it when they see it.

Crowd work and Hosting

Hosting is one of the least understood aspects of standup and much more difficult than being an act on the lineup. My first five years of standup I rarely hosted shows, which allowed me to develop a deliciously over-inflated ego surrounding my comedic abilities. When I finally did start hosting shows, I approached it with all the recklessness and overconfidence of a guy who was used to going onstage 45 minutes into a 90 minute show. In other words, comedy for me took place in a room that was already warmed up and where someone else would clean up my on-stage messes, both literal and figurative.

The reason the person hosting a show is called the host and not the first comic is because it is a distinctly different role from everyone else on the lineup. I think hosting a show is not so much different from hosting a dinner party. You don't even necessarily have to be funny (it helps), you just have to make people feel welcome and comfortable. A good host should be the most inoffensive person on the show. She or he cleans up the mess when a guest spills their drink or does something rude. The host points out the guidelines, and assures everyone that it will be ok when something awkward happens on stage (that moment after an open micer blesses the world with his groundbreaking hot take on the upside of National Socialism).

Why is crowd work called crowd *work*? Deep down comics are all very selfish and only want to do material. The crowd is there to serve as an extension of our ego and enjoy every blessed utterance that comes from a comic's mouth. But every once in a while "these people" won't cooperate and you have to engage them in conversation. To successfully do crowd work a comic must be completely in the moment. Often times honesty and transparency will pass for humor. You can also back audience members into a corner for cheap laughs. For example, *any slight hesitation* on the part of an audience member can be leveraged for a laugh. Example:

Host: Anybody here have kids?
(man in the second row raises his hand)
Host: And how old are you children sir?

Man: 3 and 5.

Host: And where are your children tonight sir?

Man: well… (thinks for a moment)

Host interjects: HEY THIS GUY DOESN'T KNOW WHERE HIS KIDS ARE!! (audience laughs) HE JUST LEFT THEM BY A DUMPSTER AND SAID "FEED YOURSELVES KIDS, DADDY'S GOING TO COMEDY!!!!" (more laughter)

Another example, this time with a couple in the front row:

Host: You guys married?

Man: Yeah.

Host: That's wonderful, how long have you been married for?

Man: ummmm ... (thinks for a moment)

Host interjects: HEY THIS GUY DOESN'T KNOW HOW LONG HE'S BEEN MARRIED FOR!! (audience laughs) OH MAN!! SOMEBODY'S IN TROUBLE!! HIS WIFE IS GOING TO LEAVE HIM BY A DUMPSTER AND SAY "FEED YOURSELF HUSBAND! I'M GOING TO COMEDY!!!" (more laughter)

This maneuver is absolutely not fair at all. People's hesitation in answering a comic's question can be for any number of reasons. Often because of the power differential in the room (the comic has a mic and they do not), they are trying to avoid getting ripped on or teased. In this avoidance, questions get answered slowly and carefully, but of course set up in the right way, this slowness can play into the host's hand.

Another trick that can add energy to the show is guessing what an audience member does for employment. This interaction can have a kind of carnival game-like quality to it. When trying to guess what a person does for a living, the host should either be exactly right or totally off the mark. It's not very funny to almost miss. For example a host asks an audience member "What do you do for a living sir?", but before the person can even begin to answer, the host interrupts and says, "No, no. Hold on! Let me guess." The host should then make a big scene out of thinking it through, as if there's some kind of deep analytical process going on in the bowels of their mind. In some contexts the host will have a pretty good shot at guessing what the audience member does. For example, a few years ago I did a show in Taiwan, where everyone in the crowd were white Americans, heavily intoxicated and drinking cheap beer. Though there is no definite way to know what a person does for a living, unless the bar is decorated (tastefully) with framed copies of audience members' pay stubs (so hip!), there is still a way to form high probability guesses. It's like playing the board game *Clue:*

[Colonel Mustard] in the [Library] with the [Candlestick] = MURDERER
[Drunk White American] in the [Asia] with the [Cheap Taiwanese Beer] = ENGLISH TEACHER

So when I said "What do you do for a living ma'am? No, no. Hold on! Let me guess… English Teacher!", people laughed and were amazed. If you do happen to guess correctly, make sure to drive home how awesome you are by saying something like, "It's not easy doing what I do, you guys are getting a real deal tonight only paying [insert door ticket price]!" In the case some clever audience member catches on to your high probability guessing scheme and yells out something along the lines of "Of course she's an English teacher!! EVERYONE here is an English teacher!!" You can bat away their annoying comment by shouting back "How am I supposed to know??? You think I'm some sorta mind reader!!?" Then quickly move on to your next joke before the magic fades.

It is also advised to take an extremely *low* probability guess with audience members. For example, a man is sitting in the front row. He clearly weighs about 55 kilos and has thick coke bottle glasses. Stereotypically, he looks like he could be in IT or work as the liberal pundit on Fox News. You say to him "What do you do for a living sir? No, no. Hold on! Let me guess… Personal Trainer!" Everyone laughs, because he's clearly *not* a personal trainer. It was one of the last things a stranger would guess him to be employed as. But now everyone is imagining what it would be like if he were a personal trainer. At this point you could contritely say "It's not easy doing what I do, what do you guys think I'm some sorta mind reader!!?" When this skinny and bespectacled nerd tells you that he is, in fact, employed in the IT industry (or that he is the reincarnated soul of Fox's Alan Colmes), you can act totally shocked as the audience laughs, thereby playing the loveable fool via the magic of comedy.

Stage presence

One of the clearest distinctions between an open micer and a professional comic is the way they stand on stage. Speaking in front of a group of people is the number one fear people have according to some surveys.[b] Because everyone has a fear of speaking in front of a group,[c] the body and the voice do things to manage this anxiety. Much like a tell in poker, this discomfort will inevitably come out in a number of ways. Some people get happy feet. They're talking on stage but keep pacing back and forth in a way that is distracting. Often people don't even know they've got happy feet. While it may not seem like that big of a deal, this pacing becomes noise and distracts from the overall perception of the performance. Audiences see this pacing and subconsciously perceive a nervousness, which also becomes noise. My tell is holding on to the mic stand. I don't know why but holding on to the mic stand, touching it and dragging it around the stage is somehow comforting to me. Sometimes holding it I look like Jack clinging to that last floating piece of wood as the Titanic is sinking to the bottom of the ocean, screaming to Rose 'Don't let go!'

With movement issues like happy feet it is essential to gain control of the body. A really helpful exercise can be to sit in a quiet place for ten minutes, focus on slow breathing and feel the sensations in the body. After feeling relaxed from deep breathing, start down at the feet and gradually work up the body focusing on each body part. Though we tend to store anxiety or psychological pain in our bodies, we're often unaware of those feelings. There may be a tightness in the shoulders or a dull pain in the stomach. These feelings may be related to external stressors. A few years ago I had a very high stress job and I would clench the right side of my jaw and grind my teeth at work. Interestingly, after a year of doing this, the hair directly above my jawline had turned white. Understanding where stress is being stored will open the door to change and greater wellbeing. This is a way that standup can be a vehicle for personal growth and development. A lot of times the fix for an on-stage issue is best resolved off-stage.

Words used while performing can also become extremely unpurposeful (i.e. noise). I've got a really bad habit of saying 'ya know' and 'right?' when feeling my way through new material.

Me: "So the other day I was at the grocery store, ya know ... and the lady working behind the counter seems like ya know she's not having a good day, right? So I'm trying to think how to…ya know.. cheer her up."

One of the most purposeful comics I've ever seen live is Ari Shaffir. Everything he does and says on stage is because he meant to. There is a feeling of confidence and control in his movements and statements. Even new material he is trying out on stage feels more polished than the best joke of a new comic, because there is no filler, either in speech or movement.

***

All stage experience is put to the test when a set is not going well. When the audience just isn't digging the jokes, every comic has the tendency, or at least temptation, to reach for verbal pacifiers. When a line doesn't work, some comics laugh nervously or look away from the audience. Some clear their throats, take a sip of water, or let out a good, "uhhhhhhh….what do I want to talk about next??" If you watch Stephen Colbert, who night after night gives an opening monologue to his show, you'll notice that some lines in that opening monologue do not land as well as Stephen and his writers probably expected. You may notice a slight change in his voice or a twinkle in his eye, but you have to look very closely because unlike newer comics, Colbert is a master of powering through when a line doesn't work well. It takes a lot of discipline to push through to the next line and act like there wasn't even supposed to be a punchline when a joke misses. But often, if the comic doesn't acknowledge it then the audience won't notice either. Colbert has confidence in his material and knows that if that last line didn't work, he'll get them with the next one.

With a little bit of discipline it's possible to power through when a line doesn't land, but the true test of stage presence is when an entire joke bombs.

Example:
Me: "Recently the entire family was devastated by the sudden passing of Oreo, the family labrador. We received a call from Aunt Connie informing us that there would be a proper burial for him at 3pm. Later that day as we were standing around the makeshift gravesite that had been dug for Oreo, everyone took a chance to say a few words. When it came time for Aunt Connie to speak, she could barely get the words out between desperate sobs. I felt really bad, so I was trying to cheer her up. I told her, 'Don't cry Aunt Connie, Oreo's in a better place now, and look on the bright side, *at least he didn't die in a Blizzard!*'"

Audience: (complete silence, judgmental looks)

The joke bombed. I've found that in these situations the best strategy is total honesty and commitment. You may want to begin by informing the audience that the joke is, indeed, over. Also, if you feel it is appropriate, take this opportunity to remind the audience that since the show has already begun, the venue is no longer able to refund their tickets. There will be murmurs of disappointment and anger, ignore these and continue with the mopping up effort. You can come clean and admit that the joke is not funny: somewhere between the applause break it got in your head earlier in the day and now, the hilarity has slipped away into the abyss. This is a viable option. People didn't pay to laugh, they paid to be entertained and public failure is one of the oldest and most revered forms of entertainment, with a rich history and tradition. Think of the hallowed days of the Roman Coliseum: people just went to see a man get his head chopped off (in other words the ancient equivalent of the Detroit Lions). Or rather, think of the warm joy that fills your heart as you watch someone else running for the bus and narrowly missing it. The audience will feel the same satisfaction as you do looking out the bus window at the out of breath person who has lost much face. Human failure is likely a comedy subcategory unto itself.

Mourn for the joke, but never apologize and never blame the audience. We all too often hear comics say, "That joke was funnier than you gave it credit for." But why are we judging the audience by this standard? In contrast, I've never heard a comic, after delivering a fresh and brilliant perspective on the inconveniences of flying economy class say, "That mediocre material was far less funny that your reaction would seem to indicate!"

You can show your total commitment to material. I enjoy hearing a failed joke followed by a detailed explanation of why it should be funny. Use phrases like "I'm playing the long game" or "That's called a comedy rope-a-dope" to convince the audience your seemingly unfunny material is part of some yet-unseen larger artistic scheme. People generally call back to their best bits, but true love is reflected in calling back to your worst bits. If you're hosting a show, you may want to take another pass at it in between comics:

Host: "Well that last guy didn't do so well ...but *at least he didn't die in a Blizzard!*"

Or even better:

Host: "Well that last guy didn't do so well ...but *at least my Aunt Connie's dog Oreo didn't die in a Blizzard!*"

When something isn't funny comics sarcastically say to each other, "You should open AND close with that!" Shock the world by taking them up on that offer. But whatever you do, whether in word or deed, do it because you meant to do it.

Notes:
[a]Generally only used with sets that are 10 minutes or longer
[b] People rated public speaking even higher than dying! However, let me assure you that both public speaking and dying at the same time are possible and available to anyone as long as they sign up at least a day in advance.
[c] I don't know if this fear has an evolutionary element to it, but if you're reading this book and trying to decide on a topic for your doctoral dissertation; you're welcome. Hopefully you are afraid to speak in front of a group of people, if not, you're not insecure enough and may be an obnoxious person – please put this book down and go take some time for self-reflection.

FOUR

The Vulnerability of a Comic

Anyone can challenge a narrative by asking why, but people won't necessarily listen. What gives the comic a special authority to question narratives? The answer lies in the vulnerability of the artform. Cloaked in hilarity and foolishness, the comic is able make statements of emotional truth or gently dismantle an idea. It is quite difficult for an audience to lash out in anger when they're laughing. Look into the neuroscience behind it, I don't believe there is a way to actively hate someone at the moment you're laughing together.

There is a childish fairness about a comedy show. The negative feedback given to the performer is instantaneous and withering. Standing alone under the hot lights, the emotionally naked comic is able to feel the harsh judgement or yawning indifference to their material. A prickly audience member may say "Challenging a narrative from the stage is not fair! The comic has a microphone!" Yes, but an audience can heckle him. It's instant judgement. This disagreeable audience member may say again, "But that's not fair either. A comic is trained to deal with hecklers!" That's true, but the real power to dismantle a show is in the audience members' hands, not the comic's. Don't believe me? Try this. If the comic is challenging your deeply held ideas and it is making you uncomfortable, stop him dead in his tracks. Go for the nuclear option of heckles: <u>the incoherent and irrelevant heckle.</u> Open up a day planner and just start reading (you don't even have to do it loudly).

Comic: ... as we were standing around the makeshift gravesite that had been dug for Oreo, everyone took a …..
Audience member: November 3. 9am drop off Dave at piano lessons. 11am. Dry cleaning at Gellagios.
TO DO: Pick up Mrs. Smitherton's medication from the pharmacy. Buy tickets to Des Moines, ask for…
Comic: Sir!
Audience member: ….[pause]….
Comic: Everything ok?
Audience member: …yeah, my bad…..
Comic: … [pause]…ehhh… everyone took a chance to say a few words. When it came time for Aunt Connie to speak, she could…
Audience member: November 4th. Have dinner with Carol.
Comic: SIR! WHAT'S GOING ON BACK THERE???

….And so on.

There are different types of hecklers, the above mentioned is referred to as a sink-hole heckler and they are the most dangerous kind. If encountered a comic should completely withdraw from them and ignore anything they do. A sink-hole heckler, though not malevolent will tie the show up in a cul-de-sac of boring conversation.

***

Comedy is like counseling: it takes two to make it go right. The comic (much like the therapist) can show the way to the door, turn the knob and open it up, but whether the audience walks through is up to them. Do they or do they not want to enter into that place called "I'm having a good time"? Or is attending a comedy show nothing more to them than hiring a human piñata for their bashing pleasure?

It takes a certain amount of generosity to run a quality show, both on the part of the comic and audience member. The best strategy is to tread lightly at first with hecklers or people zoning out. So some lady's phone went off before the punchline? Yeah, so what? Big deal! You don't know who's calling her. Maybe her grandad is in the hospital and they're calling her up with bad news. Or what about the guy in the front row who keeps getting up and walking out? You don't know. Maybe he has a rare stomach virus and keeps going to the bathroom. Or maybe he's really insecure about his girly sounding sneeze and doesn't want to get made fun of by the performer. Be gentle, who knows what emotional landmines you could be stepping on.

But the audience bears a certain responsibility to enjoy themselves as well. At some point a fair exchange has been made (people pay money in exchange for comedy) and the audience is not holding up their end of the bargain. They are stingy laughers. Just remember, grumpy audience member, comics do not provide laughter, they provide an atmosphere in which there is strong potential for laughter, nothing more. Comics entertain the audience but whether the audience enjoys themselves is up to them.

The Narcissist
There is an odd yet familiar type of audience member who will at times show up. Generally, a male between the chronological age of 40 and 60 years old (emotional age is far younger), sometimes alone yet usually accompanied by friends. This man often sits near the front and tries to dominate the room through

his gestures and words. Regardless of whether the show is going poorly or extremely well, he will make a strong effort to be the center of attention. If jokes are not landing, he will try to make them funnier by adding his own comments. If a comic is getting big laughs he will try to tear them down with heckling comments. He may also try to show his strong approval for material by giving the nod in a manner where everyone in the room can see it (e.g. yelling out "brilliant!" or clapping his hands over his head in a big way). Do not be confused by who's playing what role during the show, the comic absolutely does not need his approval. But make no mistake, he thinks he's funnier than the comic.

This kind of heckler is the most disruptive, and possibly the most dangerous in terms of ruining what would otherwise be a good show. If it were just the two of you in a room alone, then it wouldn't be a problem: let him play his imagined role of alpha male and you go on doing your thing. However, the comic's responsibility to other audience members also has to be considered. These people came to hear something, and now that is being hindered by this man's personal issues.

Assuming the performer does not have the same deep-seated narcissistic tendencies as this man, there are the following 4 options for dealing with the heckler:
Option 1. Ignore him.
Option 2. Ask the promoter to kick him out.
Option 3. Accept that the show will not be good, finish the set and get offstage.
Option 4. Create a spectacle.

My personal preference is for options two or three. Option two, if it is possible, is the best option. Yes, it will be awkward for a few minutes as he is booted from the venue. He'll hum and haw, and make a big scene. But when his presence has been removed everyone will breathe a little bit easier.

If a comic is tired or just doesn't care anymore, option three is also possible. This is where the performer lowers their head, plows through material and gets offstage as quickly as possible. This makes for a mediocre show, but who cares? There will be more shows in life. However, in a sense Options one, two and three all are a bit untrue to the craft of standup. That's because stand up is more than just telling jokes, it's a live psychological experiment with the dynamics changing from show to show.

Option one has an extremely low chance for success. The reason is that this man wants more than anything else to be the center of attention. If ignored, he will act out all the more loudly until all attention is directed at him. The only realistic way option one will end favorably for the comic is if the people around this man become exasperated to the point of shutting him down. I have seen shows like this, where one audience member loudly shouts another one down. However, that scenario also has the potential to spiral out of control. That's because narcissistic hecklers don't care about being liked, they only care about receiving attention, whether it be positive or negative.

Option 4: Create a Spectacle

Part of the reason Americans watch so much television is that our supermarkets are far too tame. You could go years without seeing a fight at grocery stores in the US, whereas in China if you hang around the Cucumber Stand for a day you'll see lots of excitement. A showdown between two people constitutes "something going down". Many expats have criticized local Chinese for being voyeuristic in their watching of "something going down". There is even a specific word in Chinese for this phenomenon – *wei guan* (围观). But this criticism is hypocritical because in reality all people worldwide enjoy this feeling of "something going down". For the purposes of better describing this phenomenon let's refer to it using the term *spectacle*. Many people will come to a comedy show with the secret hope of witnessing a spectacle. This potential for spectacle is in essence the largest difference between live performance and watching something at home. There's always a possibility of the wheels falling off when you're watching live whether it be a fight at a hockey game, a wardrobe malfunction during halftime, or just a classical concert being interrupted by a man in the wings loudly blowing his nose. This phenomenon of spectacle explains the immense popularity of *The Jerry Springer Show*. After all, what is the real difference between that show and two people aggressively haggling over a head of cabbage?

Table 3. Examples of Spectacle
1. Performer rips pants on stage
2. Audience member going into anaphylactic shock
3. Someone gets kicked out of the show
4. Gentleman in first row loudly eats a crunchy vegetable (specific vegetable unspecified)

The reason people pay money for a live performance and don't pay to go sit by the Cucumber Stand is that performances start and end at a set time. Can you imagine waiting all day in the market and not seeing anything exciting!? What a tiny payoff for so much effort. So when people come to see standup live they bare minimum expect to see a show (i.e. jokes and storytelling), but somewhere in the darkness of their little hearts they register the possibility of spectacle occurring as well.

Hence we return to the example of our arrogant heckler. If he refuses to back down and you feel the need to fulfill your duty to the other audience members (as well as to the purity of the craft), then we move to Option 4: create a spectacle. Mr. Heckler will not allow you to give them a show, therefore you choose to give them a spectacle.

Before choosing option 4 try to be sure that the heckler is not in the mafia or the chief of police of the town the show is in. Option 4 requires going all in. There will likely be no returning the show to normality after the dust settles. If you're ten minutes into a fifty minute set, you potentially sacrifice the remaining forty. It will not be pretty, but it will be memorable. People came to see a show, but if they can't have that, they will also settle for a good ole psychological showdown between two people. Mr. Heckler wants some attention, then give him *all* the attention. However, when giving him the attention your working hypothesis is that *though he wants all the attention he will not be able to hold it*. Much like the Russian armies during Napoleon's winter attack on Moscow, steadily concede psychological ground to him piece by piece. Do not attack straight away, rather allow him space and time to build the case against himself. Allow other audience members to contrast the feeling of having you in control of the room and him in control of the room. When the time comes, the weight of other audience members disapproval will be leveraged against Mr. Heckler.

In the midst of this guy's bad vibes you may feel quite intimidated. If you are fearful at this point, hold onto this truth: he is insecure and your performance is further triggering his insecurity. Do not be afraid and remember that he is afraid of you. When the room reaches a tipping point the time arrives to decide what to do with this guy, whether to harm or to heal. How to specifically go about it I can't say for sure, but I know that people tend to wear their insecurities conspicuously around them. Usually the opposite of what they're portraying is their weak point. For example if someone is flaunting wealth, they're afraid of seeming poor. If they're flaunting huge muscles, they're afraid of seeming weak. If they're overly trying to look young, they're afraid of seeming old. As a therapist, I believe it's unethical to harm with words, therefore speaking some truth into those insecurities would be my choice. This is far less gratifying than taking him down, though artistically more interesting. It's poor entertainment, but live human drama.

FIVE
Auditors of Narrative

There is nothing uniquely healthy or wise about professional therapists. People often assume that counselors are people who have all of their problems figured out. No longer riddled with anxieties and insecurities, no longer tirelessly pursued by a lurking depression, no longer strapped with financial and family difficulties, the transcendent therapist is able to reach down into the chaos of a client's life and give sage advice. This of course is an illusion. Therapists are no happier or healthier than the rest of us. When people ask me why I chose to become a counselor, I tell them grad school and a mirror was cheaper than paying for psychotherapy. I do respect the counseling profession because, in theory at least, it requires the therapist to take care of his or herself. But despite an ethical requirement of self-care, counselors do not step into the therapy session with a superior lifestyle. So if therapists are not necessarily more mentally healthy than the people they're treating, what authority do they have to work in their role?

The authority of a therapist and a stage 3 comic comes from their deep understanding of a process which analyzes and interprets narrative. Much like the mechanic who takes apart each piece of an engine and holds them in his hand, the therapist or comic is able to hold each part of a story, and understand its meaning. They take each piece of a story apart, one by one, and are able to put them back together in a more helpful way.

AUDITORS
of
NARRATIVE

SIX

The Power of Narrative

The amount of comedic material that comes from work in mental health is disappointingly low. Confidentiality aside, most of the stories heard in counseling are quite sad. People also remark how comedy must help so much when conducting a counseling session. Also not true. Strangely, the most receptivity to hearing a joke in session has been with clients coming off a recent suicide attempt. I have no idea why that's the case but if you're reading this book and trying to decide on a topic for your doctoral dissertation, you're welcome.

Comedy and counseling are two expressions of the same art form. Counseling is a craft and an art form, far less scientific than scholarly minded practitioners would like to admit to themselves. But comedy is far more scientific than comics' scores on the SAT would seem to indicate. And it all revolves around the concepts of narrative, highlighting contradictions and relationship building.

There are key differences though. People who come to therapy generally come with a desire to change, though to different degrees. The expectation is that therapy is a difficult process of self-exploration and confronting distress.[a] (However, for those who argue therapy is always more painful than comedy, I cordially invite you to attend a local open mic and sit in the audience). The central task of therapy is to show empathy, listen to the narrative of another person, and gently challenge that narrative in order to remind that person of their beautiful humanity.

A comic also challenges in order to remind the audience of their humanity. Comics give people a glimpse of the way it could be and disarm the madness of the mob with a joke and smile. Sometimes it takes a babbling fool to get people to listen to the hard truth. An undignified idiot can lower others' defenses just enough to make room for reason to peak in.

When I was a kid we had a basset hound that was constantly getting ear infections. We went to the vet and they prescribed antibiotics. The medication tasted bitter and our dog wouldn't take it, so my dad wrapped the medication in ground beef. Sometimes a comic has to wrap a message in Stage 1 ground beef to get the audience to take their Stage 3 medication. Likewise, the Fool in Shakespeare's "12th Night" is easily disregarded as mad, but if you listen closely he's making the most sense of all the characters.

In therapy one's central narrative comes out and is examined for its utility towards building a healthy and rewarding life. Sometimes what the counselor hears is an old story from the person's childhood. Their narrative may have been useful or even accurate at the age of eight, but is now outdated. The continued use of the childhood narrative is causing the adult's life to come undone. In the counseling room there is no judgement, only the cold, hard facts about 'what is my life narrative saying?' 'what is the outcome of this narrative?' and 'is this narrative helpful for me towards my goals in life?'

Mental healthcare has an extensive code of ethics, which includes not imposing one's core beliefs onto the client. Counselors create a judgement free environment in which the best interests of the client can be served. The process involves the unearthing of a client's life story so that they can examine it themselves piece by piece. The judgement of the story must come from them and not from the therapist.

Comedians however are not bound by these rules. Though the process of unpacking a story – whether it be a societal story, one's personal story, or the story of another – is the same as in counseling, comedians make judgements about these stories, sometimes in forceful and dramatic ways.

When it comes to choosing what to believe we must dispel the idea that we don't have to judge. Of course we make judgements about what to believe and we act in faith based on those judgements. One time after a show a few of the comics were driving back to the hotel and having a late night existential conversation. One remarked that "he wasn't religious", but of course I didn't believe that. I think what he meant by not being religious is that he doesn't regularly attend services at a venue of one of the major world religions or engage in activities commonly done by those religions. But I think everyone is religious in that everyone is required to have faith in a narrative of their own choosing. Some would say "I don't know what to believe", but not knowing what to believe will also require acting in accordance with that narrative.

Comics operating out of stage 3 have bravely thought through their core beliefs and they make judgements and statements based on those beliefs. Many argue that 'what you believe is good for you, and what I believe is good for me', whereas in stage 3 comics there is a higher level of commitment to their beliefs. Given their ability to break down and analyze a narrative, they advocate their beliefs to others.

No narrative is benign and every story told is a person's conception of reality. However, as is very obvious, many narratives are aggressively protected, and are not allowed to be questioned. Sometimes these narratives are protected through secrecy, violence or intimidation. Over-protected narratives are the flimsier ones, unable to stand on their own.

To exchange narratives is to enter into dialogue and in true dialogue, both parties are always changed by the other. Though you may come to think more like me or I may come to think more like you, at the end of the day I also come to see a part of me in you. The universality of being human is realised. There is a courageous commitment to truth seeking by both parties. This is very rare. Often people are interested in maintaining their own version of events, whereas seeking the truth could result in a diminishment of power or convenience. For example, one may be holding on to a terrible idea about themselves. In counseling, the three most common toxic ideas we hear from clients are: (1) I'm unloveable (2) I'm unworthy (3) I'm incompetent. These core beliefs are extremely damaging to the person, yet they cling to them! Perhaps it's all they've ever known and to believe otherwise is scary and would result in large changes to their life. Or maybe their parents told them these things about themselves and to deny it feels like a complete rejection of the parents.

Like a fish in a tank doesn't notice the water around it, many of my own narratives I took for granted. Lessons I learned from an early age about things like the redemptive quality of violence, "good" and "bad" people, and how to be a "good" person were woven intricately into my own story. My start in comedy converged with other events in life where I started to question my own beliefs. Was the timing of that questioning a coincidence or is there something inherently introspective about performing stand up? The process involved opening myself up to new ideas and engaging others in dialogue. Often engaging in real dialogue is far scarier than strongly clinging to one of these common narratives. These narratives kept the focus outward, but involved little reflection on my own behavior and attitudes.

These outward facing narratives are far more suited to the world we live in, where there are numerous apps and websites to express yourself, but not a single app that I know of for listening to others. We are used to voicing our opinion as soon as it becomes even somewhat clear in our minds, but make almost no room for doubt or time to be challenged by others' words. Dialogue puts the sharer in a vulnerable place, where it is possible for his or her beliefs to be shown as flawed, possibly convicting them to change based off of what they now know.

Notes:

[a] Or at the very least people are looking for an emotional trash receptacle into which they can verbally dump problems. In comedy this is the equivalent of being hired for a private party and then getting mercilessly heckled for 50 minutes straight. In this scenario the comic can proclaim what's happening with the statement "What do you people think this is? Some kinda kid's birthday party and I'm the human pinata? Huh? You think you can just bludgeon me and jokes will fall out?"

SEVEN

The Narratives

The Narrative of Redemptive Violence
There is a separation between my life before September 11, 2001 and my life afterwards. I cannot say I became an adult that day, but I can say it was day one of my adult life. As a senior in high school, I remember parts of that day clearly. I came out of third period gym class and someone said a plane had hit the world trade center. In fourth period we watched the towers fall on live TV.

My church called all the congregants and we held an emergency meeting that night. It was a time of sharing, venting and praying. That night I heard the word *taliban* for the first time. People were angry. There was an atmosphere of revenge in the air. I think that on September 12th an opportunity existed for humanity to make a radical change for the better, but it was not to be.

***

In the spring of 2003 I was in Texarkana, Texas during the opening days of the invasion of Iraq. The Christian college I was attending had arranged a 'campaign' (admittedly, an unfortunate choice of terminology) to go door-to-door handing out flyers inviting people to a gospel meeting. This gospel meeting was being held at the Texarkana fairgrounds, which normally showcases rodeos and livestock auctions. Four hot tubs had been brought in so that people wouldn't have to wait in line to be baptized.

The invasion of Iraq was built upon the narrative that Sadaam Hussein was funding terrorists and had begun building nuclear weapons. This narrative was somewhat weaker than the one given for invading Afghanistan, which was that Osama Bin Laden had planned and carried out the 9/11 attacks, and he was being supported by the taliban who allowed him to operate from that region. Because the story for Iraq was not as concrete and the 9/11 attacks were not so fresh, there was considerable resistance to the decision to invade. However, even in 2003 there was still more than enough anger and fear left to move ahead with a second major military campaign. At the time, myself and almost everyone I knew were totally swept up in the fervor for it. Those were the glory days of Jack Bauer of the tv show *24*. We watched that show religiously. Every time Jack pushed the moral envelope, every suspected terrorist he tortured, we cheered him on.

Now the warm afterglow from these wars has long worn off. Hollywood made an absolute event out of it. For civilians, it's difficult to think about that time period without conjuring up images from *American Sniper*, *Billy Lynn's*, and *The Hurt Locker*. Though these movies acknowledged the realities of PTSD and what soldiers go through upon returning to the US, Hollywood was kind enough to portray it in a way that we could enjoy the action (pronounced: violence) and still stomach our popcorn.

Of course now these heroic images have also become mixed with other images that do not fit so neatly into a feature film. I'm not a foreign policy or middle east expert by any definition, but with a little thought it's not hard to link the choices we made in the early 2000s with the images we see now.

The disregarded veteran, struggling to make ends meet for his family, the orphaned Syrian child, coming ashore in Greece, and the black-clad ISIL fighter standing in the back of a truck. Of course ISIL and Bin Laden did us a favor with their appearance. Men dressed in black, with beards, speaking in a foreign language are the very picture of otherness. They fit easily into a narrative given to us since childhood.

One of the earliest lessons I learned as a kid is that there are good guys and there are bad guys. Bad guys were easy to spot because they looked like bad guys. They were either deformed (Darth Vader), mentally ill (Joker), disabled (Kraige), a minority or at the very least a non-native English speaker (every James Bond movie). They were utterly inhuman and left little room for relatability. Bad guys' motivations were easy to explain, they were evil for the sake of evil. They never changed. Darth Vader didn't work out an arrangement to balance his questionable work life with family obligations, and Joker never received the loving support to help him with an obviously deep attachment issue. Because these bad guys were incapable of change and intently set on harming others for harm's sake this left the hero with no option but to resolve the conflict through violence. Conveniently, the villain's lack of relatability made it cognitively very easy to accept violence as a solution. After all, who was going to mourn the death of Darth Vader or the long-term incarceration of The Joker? These bad guys were outside of our community. Did Darth ever come and support you when a family member passed away? Was he at your side to celebrate your child's first birthday? Was The Joker ever an integral part of our friend circle?

At that time we were just kids and therefore weren't allowed to witness the close up or grisly demise of another person, regardless of their otherness. In America we have a rating system for movies and television: G, PG, PG-13 and R. Anything rated G was considered acceptable for 'General Audiences', PG meant 'Parental Guidance suggested', PG-13 indicated material that was best viewed by those above the age of 13 and R was for 'adults' (i.e. over 17). This could be viewed as a system where the amount of violence is limited for those who are younger and gradually relaxed as a child gets older and is permitted to see increasingly realistic depictions of violence. However, viewed from a different angle, this rating system could be seen as a systematic education with students graduating to higher levels and greater amounts of violent acts. So called 'Parental Guidance' in most cases amounted to the following: "It's just a movie." And so as I grew up in the US, my young mind continued to consume more murders, gradually becoming more numb to the action.

But regardless of the rating, from G to R, the narrative stayed the same. Some people can't be reasoned with, they are too far gone and must be eliminated for the good of us all. The good guys were good and always good, even their evil acts could be justified as necessary. We rarely were given the chance to gain insight into the bad guys. I can't speak for people everywhere, but I know where I grew up we tended to watch the same shows, talk about the same topics and have similar worldviews. This narrative of redemptive violence and the otherness of our enemies had so saturated our minds that when September 11 came, there was no question as to what we would do.

In 2001 I was a senior in high school. I was 17 and could legally watch rated R movies. The twin towers came down launching a global war on terror. It was graduation day.

The Narrative of 'Good People' and 'Bad People'

But for all the violence we've seen recently, let's not also fall into the trap of blaming Geoge W. Bush, Dick Cheney, Wall Street, Big Business, Weapons Manufacturers or the like. Cathartic as it is, this externalization of blame has a profound lack of creativity. This tendency to want to find the bad guy and pin blame is currently being played out at maximum volume every hour in our interconnected world.

There is an excellent book called *Hold Me Tight* written by the psychologist Sue Johnson that was required reading for our counseling graduate study. Sue Johnson is a couples therapist. In her research she found that couples in conflict engage in what she calls the demon dialogues. These demon dialogues are destructive interactions that fuel further conflict and create a nearly impossible environment to resolve fighting. One of the dialogues she termed 'find the bad guy'. An example of this is the following. A husband and wife come for therapy due to issues in the bedroom. The husband says his wife never wants to have sex and the wife accuses him of being completely unaffectionate. She says he's like an animal and only touches her when he's aroused. However, the husband has his own version of events. He says that she is an ice queen and not at all randy like she was when they were dating. I've seen couples like this in session. If you let them run a little bit it won't be long before both parties are rehashing a long list of what the other person has done. They may even try to rope the therapist in to take sides with them against their spouse.

Johnson's contribution to the field was in realising that the issue at hand is not a communication problem, but a connection problem. She based her interventions in attachment theory, which was originally written about by the British psychiatrist

John Bowlby. Bowlby's theory is that attachments created early in life will impact a person's interactions with others throughout their life. A child is born and in ideal conditions forms a strong bond with their caregiver, whether it be parents, family or other individuals. A child learns important lessons about the world via these early connections. Is the world a safe place? Can I count on others? Will someone be there to comfort me in my distress? When couples come to counseling in the midst of severe conflict, they are not necessarily divided over the issue at hand. What they are really arguing over is whether the other person will be there for them. Can they be counted on to fulfill their role and cherish their partner?

One of the first therapeutic tasks in this case is to identify this pattern of finding the bad guy. Assuming both partners share the objective of achieving a harmonious relationship, finding a bad guy and laying ultimate blame is not a viable method for conflict resolution. Inversely, listing the faults of the other increases resistance, causing them to dig their heels in deeper. Identifying the problem as something distinct from the person opens the door to admission, forgiveness and reconciliation. This is an incredibly frightening proposition for most couples. People may ask themselves "What if I release my grievances but the other person refuses to change?" This of course is a possibility, but to persist in searching for a bad guy rarely if ever results in reconciliation amongst the parties. However, for couples on the brink of a major argument taking a moment to cool down and acknowledge they are entering into a demon dance of blame can provide real breakthrough.

The demon dance in a couple's relationship is but a microcosm of the conflicts we see in the larger society. The current narrative that some people are inherently good and some people are inherently bad, enables the justification of extreme measures. It closes the door to introspection and dialogue, and dislocates people from one another.

The Russian author Aleksandr Solzhenitsyn[1] often wrestled with this question of "good people" and "bad people". He was a Soviet artillery officer in World War II. After writing letters to a friend in which he was critical of Stalin, he was arrested and spent over ten years in the Russian Gulag before eventually living in exile. On this particular issue he wrote:

"If only there were evil people somewhere insidiously committing evil deeds, and it were necessary only to separate them from the rest of us and destroy them. But the line dividing good and evil cuts through the heart of every human being. And who is willing to destroy a piece of his own heart?"

***

I used to love reading the newspaper. My main motivation for reading the newspaper were the following: a) to see if The End of The World was imminent (e.g. stock market crash, nuclear disaster, Lions playoff run), b) sometimes they publish interesting recipes, like how to make a flaming cake or cook salmon using only olive oil and cornflakes, and c) reporting of a scandal and the subsequent downfall of a person in leadership.

I must admit that I have such a deep sense of the world's unfairness that I love to read about some white collar banker or high up politicians getting caught breaking the law. This feels like a gotcha moment where justice is going to get served. In some ways the punishment doesn't even matter to me, it's more about the truth being out in the open. But lately I rarely can bring myself to read the newspaper, let alone turn on the TV or take a peek at Twitter. It's an endless purging of bad people being swallowed up by the maw of the machine. Who these bad people are largely depends a lot on what news source one goes to.

Humans are meant to live life connected to those around them. It is hardwired into our biology. An interesting example is a study by Coyne et al. (2001)[2] examining people's life expectancy after a major heart attack. Their results found that those who had a loving relationship with their partner generally outlived those who rated their relationship as poor or stressful.

For couples, continuing to find the bad guy results in divorce (whether it be of the legal or emotional kind), so why should the result be any different in a society? In fact with social and news media this societal divorce has already happened, where we don't have to deal with the thorny issues of relationship to one another.

The power of comedy, as with couples counseling, is in its vulnerability and simplicity. A counselor will first try to identify this 'find the bad guy' pattern and name it. She or he will try to bring the two people together to find their commonalities. Comics, through the mechanism of laughter and narrative can also bring people together.

The desire for justice and to be in the right is so strong. During my ten years in China I often strongly wished for bad people to get what was coming to them, all the while believing myself to be a good person. However, as my years in China went by, the personal narrative of my own goodness became more and more difficult to justify. There was something emotionally inauthentic about it. It reached a point where I began to look for a way out.

References:

1. Solzhenitsyn A.I. *The Gulag Archipelago* (1973) Harper & Row, New York

2. Coyne James et al., *Prognostic importance of Marital Quality for survival of congestive heart failure*, (Am J Cardiol 2001;88:526–529)

EIGHT
The Factory

The initial idea to live outside of the US began when I was twelve and my dad took a trip to Panama. Dad was a welder and went as part of a team that was digging wells in rural areas. He came back from Panama with strange currency and interesting stories. A few years later I took my first trip out of the US to Honduras. I was there for two weeks and when I came home my biggest passion became seeing the world.

I wanted to see as many places as possible and be wise about how the world is. The worst thing I could imagine was to be naive. I greatly admired those people like Ernest Hemmingway: well-traveled, world weary and cynical. I imagined myself one day to be like the protagonist in a Hollywood spy film: working in some impoverished, war-torn region, returning home depressed and addicted to cheap bourbon (so glamorous!)

Unwise as it may seem, I've always chosen jobs based on whether or not I thought that job would yield cool stories. One time I had two job offers: one was working as a recruiter of English teachers, the other working as quality control guy in a rural factory in central China. Initially, I decided to take the recruiting job. My first day at that job was so painfully boring that I quit after one day. Being bored sucks. I called the other company to see if the factory job was still available and they said it was. My first week at that job half of the factory burned to the ground. I knew I had made the right choice.

***

It is true that half of the factory burned to the ground but luckily no one was injured. It's not clear how the fire started, all we know from reports on the ground is that there was a worker doing some welding (without a mask) near a gas line. He was welding. He was smoking a cigarette while welding. He was near a gas line. But after an extensive investigation it was determined that the fire started for unknown reasons.

I worked there for over a year and was under a little bit of stress. We were manufacturing packaging materials for a men's grooming company. Our packaging was part of a green initiative because the packs were made of one hundred percent renewable fibers (bamboo, bullrush, and sugarcane) that would completely decompose after being discarded. The packs that were being produced came in two colors and we were to produce 100,000 pieces a day. Of course it's a little tricky to make so many pieces when half of your facility is a firepit. Our packaging was also the centerpiece of a new product launch that this company was doing. There was immense pressure to deliver shipments on time, so we had nightly conference calls with people on the line from China, Europe, and the US. I was tasked with getting this manufacturing effort back on track. Our CEO liked to tell customers that we had "boots on the ground" and the nightly conference calls would start with a report from "our man on the ground in China" on how many pieces had been made that day. It was a multi-million dollar project and a lot of pressure for a guy in his late twenties whose college major was Spanish[a], not engineering or business.

I'm not very good at math and never have been. In high school I failed my freshman algebra class and had to take it over again as a sophomore. After I passed freshman algebra as a sophomore I never took another math class again. I don't know how you can graduate high school having only taken a year of math, it's a testament to the public school system in Michigan. But I do know how to round up numbers. For example the number 0.5 rounds up to 1. But according to my limited knowledge of math 8 or 9 thousand does not round up to 100,000 in most cases. On these nightly conference calls, to make the daily production numbers work, a more advanced statistical method called 'massaging the numbers' was required. Doing such difficult math required a lot of intellectual and moral energy from me, which was stressful.

In addition to these math problems there were other issues such as the supposedly 'green' product we were making for use in Europe and the US was ruining the local environment in China. This is the big dirty secret of the green packaging industry. While a renewable fiber salad bowl can indeed be thrown into a compost pile and broken down, the reality is that this final product is the result of dirty manufacturing and cheap labor on the supply side. Factories in China and Southeast Asia are running round the clock on dirty coal energy to make these bowls, which are then shipped to far away markets using more fossil fuels to get them there. It's good to want to do something for the planet, but probably the greenest decision is just to consume less. Buy one nice bowl and just use that one bowl for the rest of your life. When it's dirty, wash it.

To make a completely green product requires manufacturing to happen on a closed loop system where nothing is wasted. This process is possible, but expensive and makes products too expensive for the average American consumer to accept. In the remote areas where a lot of these packages are made, important safety measures are overlooked for expediency. The process for making our product required massive amounts of water. If an auditor were stopping by the factory, they would see water being used in the process and then being treated on the back end to minimize environmental damage. Of course what happens in a factory on audit day is quite different than normal operation. One of our premier packages was blue. It used a blue dye to color the bamboo/sugar cane/bulrush pack. There was a river that ran through the middle of the small town where our facility was located. One day I went down to the river and to my horror saw that the river was the exact same blue color as the dyes we were using. I notified the plant manager who went down to the river with me. He didn't seem to think the color was because of the dyes. "It's blue. Water is blue," he told me.

At that time I was reading a book called *Poorly Made in China*. The author was just like me, a China guy who started doing business in the manufacturing sector. I thought the guy was so awesome, he was exactly what I was trying to be: a guy who had seen things, was well-traveled, world weary and cynical. Spoiler alert about that book, the guy had a heart attack in his mid thirties and almost died from stress.

When I was stressed I would grind my teeth or clench the right side of my mouth. I had weird nightmares and would wake up in the morning with a sore jaw. Feel free to draw your own conclusions about why I held anxiety in my jaw. My favorite theory is that the jaw is the place where the head and the mouth meet. At that time there was a disconnect between what I knew was right in my head and what I was willing to speak out against. Because I kept my mouth shut more days than not, that tension all collected in my jawline and temples.

***

In addition to being dirty, the factory was just an all around unpleasant and dangerous place. Local people would travel the mountain roads from up to an hour away to come to work. It was common to see fatal traffic accidents on those roads, but luckily I took out excellent life insurance.

I always pictured factories employing brawny, mean faced men, but actually most of the people working there were young women between the ages of 16 and 25. There were two 12 hour shifts and people would work in the summertime in over ninety degree heat stopping only once for lunch or dinner depending on the shift.

There was a lot of travel involved with this job as well. In addition to being in China, I was regularly going to Europe to meet with our customers and explain why orders were falling behind and why the quality of the products was so miserably low. The facility in Europe was large and modern, the people working there were professionally trained engineers and I think it would have blown their minds to see our rebuilt firepit in central China. Because a lot of our product had been declared 'rejects' we got into a situation where the amount of money we owed to our customer continued to climb. On one trip, I had just arrived when the facility manager called me into his office and angrily told me that we owed them $750,000 because the previous shipment had been so bad.

The bosses in Europe were jerks, but the engineers were pretty nice to me. I think they had pity on me because they knew I wasn't good at math. Each time I visited their facility, they would patiently explain to me what I needed to do to train the workers in China so that product quality wouldn't be so bad. I vowed to return, train up the team and resolve the situation as quickly as possible.

But inevitably my American bosses had other ideas about what "training" should look like and that usually amounted to ratcheting up the pressure on people so that product came out faster and rejects wouldn't find their way to our customers. I would yell at people in meetings and angrily dump over boxes on the factory floor in front of workers to make sure my point was made. They told me, "Make sure when you're done yelling to throw your hat. That lets them know you're serious!"

I jotted down some notes on their management techniques and am confident this material could be added to the curriculum of any culturally-sensitive MBA program:

Table 4. Management techniques for cross-cultural communication, team building, efficiency, and morale
1. Kick more ass, take no prisoners w/ authority
2. Find their Achilles heel and pound away
3. Play to win/Win to play/Eat their lunch/Get in their head
4. Last man standing and a trail of dead bodies ("Turn up the pressure on these guys!")
5. SCREAM, etc.*

*'Screaming at people' is not technically an engineering method, it's more quasi-science, similar to 'massaging the numbers'.

***

During this period I can't imagine I was much fun to be around. Tired, stressed, in way over my head, I started turning to unhealthy means of managing life. Every business trip involved a visit to the airport duty free store because I reckoned myself a bit of a whiskey connoisseur at that time. I amassed quite an impressive alcohol collection: old bottles of Laphroig, rare editions of Glenkinchie, and tasty Polish bison grass vodka.

There's a tendency to look back and think of periods of life as the good old days. We had late nights and wild parties sometimes. Dinners with customers were always at fancy places and put on the expense accounts. It smooths over the awkwardness with customers and auditors to know that you'll all be enjoying a steak dinner later that night. I guess it was a big party, like an extension of college. Looking back I can see it was an illusion as well. The reality was that I spent a lot of time alone, trying to fix unfixable problems by pressuring and manipulating the people around me.

***

Staying in hotels is really cool, I love how you can leave in the afternoon and come back at night to find that tiny elves have made your bed. I stayed at some pretty sweet places and when the regular rooms were booked I got upgraded to the executive suite that had a hot tub.

I stayed at some really lousy places too. The small factory town only had one hotel which the factory manager called The Obama Hotel, because "if Obama ever came to town, this hotel is where he'd stay". It was little more than a countryside house with multiple rooms. It had a squat toilet under the shower and huge roaches. I slept in my clothes because roaches would climb up onto me while I slept at night. Not that I got a lot of sleep at the Obama Hotel, because of course the nicest hotel in town also doubled as a brothel/gambling den. The walls were paper thin and you could hear customers in the room next door with prostitutes or drunken men playing mahjong until 6 o'clock in the morning.

However the hardest part of this job was managing others' expectations of me and how it impacted my self-esteem. I wasn't an engineer or a product developer. I was presented as the China Guy, a vague designation that gave the impression I knew how to navigate the complexities of working in rural supply chain management, when in fact my mandarin was mediocre and my understanding of rural Chinese working culture was limited at best. This made me so insecure that I would shake in my seat during meetings, terrified that someone would call on me to translate. Translation errors were costly too, saying something just a little bit inaccurately could result in the loss of tens of thousands of dollars.

Two translation errors in particular stick out in my mind. One happened my first day on the job. I was negotiating what my salary would be with the company and during one of the final interviews, the VP of the company dialed up the factory and asked me to speak with them. A particular product had quality issues. Blue dots were appearing on the pack after they came out of the machine but the packs were supposed to be completely orange. My soon-to-be boss got them on the line, handed me the phone and said, "Ask them why the blue spots are appearing on the pack." I was super nervous to be put on the spot and was stuttering to the person on the other end of the phone. For the life of me I couldn't think of how to say blue dot in Chinese.*

[in case you care, the word for blue dot is 'lan dian' (蓝点), but they called them black spots 'hei dian' (黑点)]

As the VP scrutinized me I continued to nervously mutter into the phone for a minute until I shamefacedly handed the phone back to him and said, "I'm sorry, I don't know the word for blue dot." I ended up accepting their initial salary offer, which was lower than I was hoping for.

The second translation error cost me my job. After a year of working there, production started to stabilize. I didn't have to do so much number rounding anymore. But product quality was still a point of sharp conflict between the China side and our customers. The factory manager, who spoke no English, took a trip out to Europe and I was to go with him as a translator. During this trip we reviewed their manufacturing processes and were able to see first-hand how our product quality was impacting their production. In meetings we worked out a deal where the China side would agree to a no more than 0.1% defect rate for all deliveries. If the rates were over this, a financial penalty would have to be paid. Everyone seemed pleased with this agreement and we left the next day to head back to China.

But all hell broke loose the next month when the customers sent us a bill for a shipment with a 0.8% defect rate. There were angry phone calls and emergency meetings called between our US bosses and the China-side leadership. The exact point of contention was that our European customers understood all shipments to not have a defect rate above 0.1% whereas the guys at the factory in China had understood that number to be 1.0%. While it may not seem like a huge difference, the production of renewable fiber packaging is an extremely inexact process. Given our facility and the near ancient machinery we were using, a rate of 0.8% was about as good as it would get. The

China management was outraged. Further improvement would require a major investment and overhaul of the factory. If that were the case there'd be no way to remain profitable and they may as well stop working tomorrow.

Of course we had talked about all of this during our trip to Europe, but it was just me and the China manager. It was his word against mine and honestly who is going to trust a guy who doesn't even know the word for blue dot? I already had a rapidly deteriorating relationship with the manager, I felt he used me at times as a scapegoat to cover over the factory's mistakes. But my relationship with my American bosses wasn't great either, they liked to use me as a missile to launch their frustrations against the factory boss. I had been caught in the middle of two warring factions for over a year and felt burned out. Moreover, I hadn't brought peace to the situation, but made it worse with my own power plays and manipulation.

In that final meeting about the 0.8% defect rate everything came to a head for me. All the major players were at the meeting to discuss just where the lines got crossed in the communication. During the meeting my blood was boiling as the blame got passed around, with the heftiest portion coming to me. The factory boss kept deflecting everything to the trip we had taken to Europe. He said the miscommunication was my fault, my Chinese was bad, and I didn't know anything about business or manufacturing. It was so humiliating.

I'm not super familiar with the backstory of where the term 'scapegoat' comes from. I think it comes from ancient Greek times where if one of the younger members of a clan made an accounting error at work, the elder members of the clan would get HR to fire a goat. Nevertheless, it became clear to me during this meeting that they were looking for a scapegoat and consensus was beginning to settle on me. I started to panic, and in my moment of panic I reached deep down into my soul for something I could use: some kind of wisdom or strategy, some deep spiritual mantra to elevate me out of the present darkness and into a safe space. Then the clouds in my mind began to part and I found my answer: the management techniques that my bosses had taught me.

Boy did I give them a piece of my mind! I yelled and cursed and ranted! There weren't any hats or boxes around to toss, but I think it was ok.

After the stunned silence in the room began to fade away, my boss was the first to speak. I can't recall his exact words, something about cordially inviting me to leave the meeting and don't let the door hit me in the ass on the way out, cause I was fired.

Notes:

[a] I spent 9 years and $80,000 studying Spanish and then upon graduation promptly moved to a country of 1.5 billion people, and about 6 of them spoke Spanish.

NINE

The Conditional Love of a Comedy Show Audience

Near the end of my time at the factory I discovered this thing called standup comedy. My first set ever was part of a larger variety show. I had planned to do a comedic cover of the Greenday song "Time of Your Life" talking about my recent experience of meeting Hillary Clinton. Unfortunately, the guy who went on before me did a twenty-minute spoken word, slam poetry-eulogy to Chilean novelist Roberto Bolaño.

This guy wasn't exactly getting the audience hot and bothered for some comedy. By the time I went up the audience was bored and confused (and like many of you asking yourselves "Who the hell is Roberto Bolaño?") In scenarios such as this, a show will tend to wildly veer one way or the other. If it veers badly, the audience gives up on the show, shuts down and starts looking at their watches. Anything funny will fall on deaf ears. However, it can also break the other way, people may be so relieved to hear some comedy and lightheartedness after a eulogy that they get behind your jokes in a big way.

Luckily for me my set broke the second way with the audience. After twenty minutes of such obscure high-brow gobbledee goop, they lapped up the easily digestible three chord comedic cover. The set was the highlight of the show and a couple comics from the local scene were in the audience. They came up to me afterwards and asked if I'd be interested in doing open mic.

Probably the best advice I could have received at that time would have been to love comedy but not to let it define my identity. Comedy is a journey worth taking, whether it be for a period of a few months or a lifetime. One can enjoy the stimulation and satisfaction that comes from doing it well. Even when done poorly, comedy can provide material for self-reflection and development. But a person's identity is sacred. It's something very intimate and needs to be responsibly protected. One of the biggest risks that can be taken on stage is to share one's identity with others. Allowing comedy to define identity opens up a dangerous path. The truth is comedy audiences are often fickle and stupid. People come to be entertained and often have little understanding of the vulnerability it takes to go on stage. Like children in a museum, audiences will trample your work of art – which in comedy is experiences and thoughts – if you let them.

When I started doing comedy, the scene in Shanghai was nothing like it is now. There were only a few comics and shows were a couple of times a month, whereas now there are hundreds of people and comedy is happening somewhere every night of the week. The audiences were quite virginal in those days. Anything said with even the slightest whiff of humor got huge laughs. It was a potent and deadly mixture for me—audiences were hungry to laugh and I was hungry to be good at something. My time at the factory coincided with starting out in comedy. I felt so incompetent at that factory, but doing shows on the weekends I finally felt like there was something I could control. When you put your heart into the audience's hands and they love you, the feeling is addictive. All the love and self affirmation you could ever hope for comes in that moment. The buzz lasts for several days. But when I gave them my heart and it went badly, I would be devastated. Self doubts and insecurity pushed me to manipulate the relationships around me. It became all about me.

It took me a long time to realize it, but the affirmation you get from comedy is a very conditional form of love. There's pressure to be a certain way and talk a certain way. You are only as valuable as what you produce. Depending on the scene, it can be a hypercompetitive environment. Some say that this kind of environment weeds out the losers and increases performance quality. I don't necessarily disagree with that idea. However, I now know that denial of others inherent value based on narrowly defined criteria tends to homogenize a scene, thereby reducing its diversity and creativity.

TEN

You're Not a Catcher Anymore

Before getting canned from the factory, I took one last solo business trip to Europe. I packed several books and prepared for lots of alone time in airports and hotels. I had begun to read a lot more about the field of psychology.

This was because when my jaw grinding started, I went to see a physician because of heart palpitations. He told me there was nothing wrong with me physically, I was just stressed out and should consider seeing a therapist.

The therapist I saw was a wonderful man. In one session I had made a passing reference to my impressive duty free whiskey collection. He made a mental note and later asked me how much regular drinking I did. I told him not a whole lot, to which he knowingly smiled. This counselor suggested I take two weeks off from drinking and see how I feel. "I'm not here because of a drinking problem" I told him. "Good", he said, "then it shouldn't be that difficult to take a break."

If you've ever seen Ghostbusters, there's that scene where they have all the ghosts locked in a box down in the basement. At one point in the movie somebody goes and opens the box, letting all the ghosts out. Taking time off drinking felt a bit like opening that box. You don't have to be a diagnosable alcoholic to use booze to manage the unpleasant but very normal realities of life. (Or as I like to call it, gently sanding the rough edges off existence). It was an absolutely eye opening experience, but not easy.

I proudly went back to therapy two weeks later, having not drank and told him "You see! I told you drinking wasn't a problem for me!" He just smiled and said, "That's great! So it definitely won't be a problem to do *another* 2 weeks!" He was so clever. That second 2 weeks was so difficult, but the turning point in my therapy.

After 9 months of seeing this counselor we were getting ready to terminate.[a] He told me in one of our last sessions "You're pretty good at this, you should try being a counselor." This guy inceptioned me. I started thinking about what it would be like to be a professional therapist. After all, they say that psychology is far easier than math.

***

I considered myself a bit of a so-called China expert by the end of my time working at the factory. But looking back now I can see that getting fired from that job was the real start of my China education. The factory boss was pissed because I cursed his mom and made him lose face in front of the whole team. It didn't matter that he had frustrated and made me look stupid numerous times as well. This wasn't a relationship of equals in his mind. And so by getting fired I learned an important lesson. There are many laws in China, but only one rule: Don't make trouble. This realization would come to serve me well in my next phase.

For 6 months I was unemployed, staying in Shanghai, trying to figure out my next move. I had a lot of time to reflect on my life and where it was all going. I started dabbling in church and prayer again, something I hadn't touched much since college. At that time I also got really into the movie *Moneyball*. If you've never seen *Moneyball*, it's the story of Billy Beane, the general manager of the Oakland A's baseball team. The A's are a small market team with a budget that's not big enough to hire superstar baseball players, so they're constantly losing to large market teams like the New York Yankees and Boston Red Sox. As Billy says early in the movie "[baseball] is an unfair game." The team's inherent disadvantages lead Billy to search out radical new methods for trying to win. He and his team develop a system for evaluating players in a way that no one else had done before. In this new system they could see the good in people, that others couldn't clearly see. Because other teams couldn't see how good these players actually were, they undervalued them and the A's were able to hire these players using their small budget and build a playoff team with almost no money.

That movie resonated deeply with me in a way no movie had before. Not only was Billy changing the way baseball was played, he was changing the way people saw others. There was one scene in the movie where during the offseason Billy wants to hire Scott Hadeburg, who was an elite catcher who had just undergone career ending surgery on his elbow. If a catcher can't throw, he's no longer able to play. But Billy wants to hire Scott to play first base, because he's figured out there are other strengths Scott has which are even more useful to the team. Maybe this scene in the movie struck a chord because it reminded me of my own situation. Billy goes over to Scott's house during the holidays. There's Scott sitting on the couch, unemployed and slightly depressed. Much to Scott's surprise he's offered a contract to do something he's never done before. He seems unsure of this new offer, to which Billy bluntly says "Scott, you're not a catcher anymore." This statement must have struck deep at his identity, but the offer of a new contract also brought a hope for the future.

For that half a year of being unemployed I felt like Scott and God was my Billy Beane. I kept going to interviews looking for other factory jobs, trying to stick to what I knew. The interviews were usually a disaster, sometimes laughably so. In one interview they dragged me into a conference room and had the secretary speak to me as fast as she could to see if I understood Chinese. She sounded like an auctioneer, and I think it annoyed her when I responded in a purposely slow and stupid sounding voice. In another interview the boss, who was American, admitted that his management style basically amounted to verbally abusing his employees. (He must have attended the aforementioned MBA program). That particular interview was at nine at night, and I knew I didn't want to work there when I saw all of his exhausted looking employees were still there, toiling away in front of their computers. Another manufacturing job I didn't get because I took too many notes during the interview. That particular instance I was basically interviewing them, asking very specific questions that were references to my previous job. I'm sure my very specific questions had the feel of someone going on a date when they haven't really gotten over their ex.

It wasn't that I really wanted to get another factory job, it was just something familiar. A lot of people tolerate bad situations or relationships because they're familiar. Though they could do a lot better, it's hard to imagine anything different. Throughout this whole period I kept thinking to myself, maybe I'm not a catcher anymore. Perhaps the factory had done the occupational equivalent of blowing out my throwing arm and it was time to move on. After many failed attempts at finding a new factory job, I decided to give up.[b]

That tiny voice in the back of my head kept working on me, telling me to take a leap of faith and go into the mental health field. It was a little bit tricky in China though. For one, to get into the mental health field you need a graduate degree, which I didn't have. To get a graduate degree, you have to go back to school, which as far as I knew China didn't have any programs in English. But over time I noticed a pattern: first take a risk, and confirmation about that decision doesn't come until much later.

So I started looking around for opportunities just to understand what it might be like to work in mental health. Someone suggested that I should volunteer at Lifeline, which is the crisis hotline for expats in Shanghai. You had to go through a couple of weekend trainings, so I signed up and went. When I arrived at the training a lady was greeting people at the door. I introduced myself and within about a minute of talking we found out that, improbably, we had both lived in the same tiny town in central China – Jingzhou. I was in Jingzhou my first year in China, working as an English teacher at the local petroleum engineering college. I was living there in 2007 and at that time there were only 6 non-Chinese persons living in the whole town. This woman and her husband, a psychiatrist, were living there in the nineteen eighties, running a ward at the local mental hospital. This woman was the trainer for the crisis hotline and we struck up a friendship that would change the course of my life.

I don't know if volunteering at Lifeline was more a lifeline for the people I was supposed to be helping or for myself. After the training, I began my shifts there, which involved sitting in a booth alone waiting for the phone to ring. It was quite an unnerving experience. It was so quiet in that booth and when people called it could literally be regarding any issue. Maybe they were a little sad because their cat had just died, or maybe they were severely suicidal and you had to talk them out of ending their life on the phone. One regular caller used to masturbate over the phone. I wish this person the best in life, but honestly I was glad when they decided to block her number. Truthfully, the phone didn't ring much at all. Shifts were 4 hours long and everyone was required to do a minimum of 2 shifts a month.

I started in January and by March had only fielded a handful of calls. I would dutifully show up to my shifts, sit in the booth reading books about psychology alone and wait for the phone to ring. I was starting to get pretty discouraged. Maybe this venture into mental health was just another dead end and I should start wholeheartedly looking for a factory job again. I resigned myself to this and started going back to those idiotic factory job interviews. But every interview was just another door slamming shut.

I called up my friend the trainer and we went out to grab lunch. I despairingly told her how frustrated I was with my situation and pouted that I'd never get to work in the mental health field. Her husband was still working as a psychiatric researcher and she graciously invited me over for dinner to see if he could find some odd jobs I could do around his office. I guess having completed my time with the psychologist it was time to go see the psychiatrist.

Things started to happen quickly. Around that time, I also received a call from my former therapist. He said Palo Alto University was opening a graduate counseling program in China and would I be interested in applying? The school is one of the top psychology colleges in the US, located near the campus of Stanford (you've heard of osmosis). They saw the value in training the next generation of therapists in China and were looking for a pioneering batch of students (kind of like The

Oregon Trail of mental health). While preparing to apply I went to go have dinner at my friend's house. Though I didn't know it at the time, her husband is a legend in the mental health field in China. He came as a young doctor in the late seventies (the Pong of mental health) and was a part of China's burgeoning field of psychiatry. I was intimidated talking to this man who would soon become my mentor. I didn't see why he would need me, a Spanish major with a few years of English teaching experience, working at his mental health research center. He told me to come by the next day and I could check out the center.

Early the next morning (it happened to be April Fool's Day), I set off for the far southern suburbs of the city. His office was located on the satellite campus of the Shanghai Mental Health Center. This hospital was originally built in the 1930s by German missionaries and at that time named Mercy Hospital. It is a sprawling 3000 bed hospital, with spacious lawns and many of the original buildings maintained over the years. There is an old chapel in the center of the campus that is now being used as a rehabilitation unit. It looks exactly how you would imagine the old timey insane asylums to look, like a scene out of *Shutter Island*. The research center occupies the second floor of a two story building, the first floor being a rat lab for animal studies. My initial feeling was that I was in way over my head, going to a place in China few foreigners had seen and possibly being a part of something I had neither the qualifications or the background for. When I walked into his office, the doctor was expecting me. He said "I thought about it last night, and I think I need somebody full time, when's the earliest you can start?" Though I was initially suspicious about this job because nothing burned to the ground during the first week, I decided to start working there.

Notes:

[a] In counseling 'termination' means therapy is coming to an end and is nothing at all like when Neo gets that tube pulled out of the back of his head.

[b] A message about giving up: People love to post and quote inspirational sayings about never giving up. Winston Churchill said such and such. Winston Churchill with his cigar hanging out of his jowels standing over a bombed out shopping center said don't give up on yourself. Winston Churchill's famous drunken graduation speech, "Never give up. Never give up. Never give up!" You know what though? Winston Churchill was fighting THE SPECTRE OF A NAZI WORLD TAKE OVER, not battling to open the third combination latte shop-yoga studio in Oshkosh, Wisconsin! Why do you even need to open another combination latte shop-yoga studio? This town already has two! So what I'm trying to say is, if life is leading you down the wrong path, give up as quickly as possible.

ELEVEN

Doctor Fralick

In my new work environment I went from being surrounded by farmers turned migrant factory workers and sleazy businessmen to doctors, experts in biostatistics (whatever that means) and PhD level professionals in mental health and economics. Everyone around me just assumed I was a doctor too, so they started calling me Doctor Fralick. I sheepishly tried to explain to them that I was just a guy, but eventually I gave up. My first month on the job I got to tag along for a conference held at the Harvard Center for Global Health about the future of mental healthcare in China. On the one hand, I was fascinated by all the exciting topics and projects being talked about, but on the other I was stunned by these high-level professors' optimism about the situation on the ground in China. I still carried around all the cynicism that had grown on me from my time at the factory. This cynicism was a badge I wore to protect me from the insecurity I felt being in this new environment.

My first job at the hospital was as assistant editor for a peer-reviewed psychiatry journal. Over the past ten years, China has ramped up efforts to become a powerhouse in the area of published research. As part of this effort all doctors are encouraged to publish research in an SCI journal, in addition to their clinical and administrative duties. SCI, the Science Citation Index (disparagingly referred to as the Stupid Chinese Idea) is a database of elite science journals, kind of like a Google that selects only the top sources globally from each field of study.

Publishing in SCI is a world unto itself. Under China's healthcare system, doctors who are being considered for a raise or a promotion are put under heavy scrutiny, with publication of research factoring heavily into whether or not they can advance in their careers. The standards for acceptance of a research study into an SCI journal are much higher than other journals and for China's doctors the ability to get their papers in SCI could make or break them professionally. This has led to an environment where the psychiatrists in charge of the mental health wards are the most well published, but not necessarily the most clinically gifted or empathic.

China had no SCI journals in the field of mental health. Our task at the journal office was to improve the quality of articles we published and increase our readership, thereby making us an appealing applicant for SCI inclusion.

***

As I continued over the next couple of years plugging away at manuscripts for our journal, I was also getting deeper into my graduate studies. In the final year of the three year master's program every student has to do a supervised clinical internship. Because of my job at the hospital, I had access to the wards, which provided the potential for a unique internship. One day I asked one of my colleagues if I could sit in on a group therapy session that she was leading. The ward she was working on was an all female unit for chronic mental illness. Many of the patients had been living there for ten or even twenty years.

In the US, mental healthcare transitioned into community treatment in the 1960s. Large psychiatric hospitals were closed down and treatment was focused more on an outpatient basis. What this meant in practice was that a lot of patients had to fend for themselves. It's not uncommon to see homeless people on the streets of American cities who clearly have some kind of psychiatric condition. In China, however, those with severe mental illness are often hospitalized long-term.

Many of the clients I saw during my internship were people whose family were financially or otherwise unable to care for them. In low and middle-income countries, where the line between making it and poverty is so thin, the onset of a serious mental disorder in someone can bankrupt their entire family. In these cases, patients may essentially become wards of the state. For long-term inpatients, their whole world and community were inside the four walls of the mental health center. Some were quite contented to be living in this environment, while others had given up hope of life on the outside as they slowly became institutionalized.

My first time attending that therapy group for the women, I was quite intimidated. There were about twelve women in the group. They were of all ages and had varying levels of coherence. I recall one woman attended the group after having just undergone ECT (electroconvulsive therapy, or as it's commonly known 'electroshock therapy') and had no idea where she was, due to the side effects of the treatment. Because this ward was in one of the older buildings at the hospital there was no dedicated room to have meetings in, so we improvised by meeting in one of the large storage rooms. It was quite an odd scene, 12 Chinese female patients, a psychiatrist and one white male intern sitting in a circle talking. The janitors had no concept of what group therapy was and would periodically come in to grab a mop or some cleaning supplies. We had to remind them not to come in while we were in there because sessions were supposed to be confidential. They just shrugged and kept rummaging around for the Lysol, or whatever it was they were looking for.

In the beginning, I was mainly an observer in the therapy group. A few weeks into the group, the psychiatrist I was working with told me she had other commitments at that time going forward. She asked if I would be able to lead the group starting next week. That was my first real gig as a counseling intern. Every week I would nervously lead the group, constantly in amazement at the turn my life had taken. Who thinks growing up in Midwestern America that one day you'll be leading a women's therapy group in a mop closet at a state run hospital in China?

There is this idea every young therapist has that you have to 'do something' to help the people you see. It's not until later that one learns just to be with people. I learned that there is tremendous therapeutic power in groups. Many of these patients came from broken families. The older women had strained relationships with their children and the younger patients had difficulties with their parents. In China, the stigma against mental illness is destructive to the point that being admitted to a psych unit can derail a person's path to having a career, a partner, or a family. Though in 2012 the first ever national mental health law was passed, not much emphasis was given to combating stigma. There is a lot of shame attached to having common conditions like depression and anxiety, though that shame is even greater for illnesses involving psychosis like schizophrenia or bipolar disorder. Common insults heard in the streets are *'shen jing bing'* (you are mental ill), *'nao zi huai le'* (your brain is broken), or *'ni you bing!'* (you're sick!). For these women, those words cut to the bone.

But I also found the psych ward, in some ways, to be one of the sanest places I've been to. In Asian cultures communication is often happening on multiple levels. Something said to another person can often be vaguely worded, with multiple possible meanings, and it's up to the listener to decipher what the speaker is trying to say. Relationships are complicated as well and operate by an unspoken set of cultural rules. There is a clear hierarchical distinction made early on in interactions between who is higher in the relationship and who is lower. Once the distinction is made the relationship usually continues to operate within that framework. To have mental illness is to always be slotted into that lower position relationally. People with mental disorders are at best disregarded and at worst feared by those around them. However the ward was an environment free of this pretense. People were there because they had an issue and this dynamic created an equality that fostered honest and straightforward conversations. In the ward there was no need to pretend.

As the group continued its course over the next several months I noticed a healthy pattern developing. The older women were able to compassionately mentor those younger women. They all shared stories and experiences from their lives, and were respectfully listened to and accepted. For the younger women, they were able to receive a type of motherly love and concern from those older ladies, and the older ladies seemed to find healing in nurturing the younger group members. All of the therapeutically useful parts of this group were happening completely independently of anything I, the "expert", was adding to the group.

My internship got into full swing when I started seeing patients for one-on-one counseling sessions. The majority of my client load in the first year was working with women who had chronic schizophrenia. When many people think of mental illness the first image that comes to mind is of the howling mad psych patient, floridly psychotic, seeing things that aren't there, hearing voices in their head, or having bizarre delusions about themselves and the world. The therapeutic method for helping someone with extreme delusions is quite counterintuitive. Let's take for example a case where the patient strongly believes themselves to be John the Baptist. This is not an actual example from my clinical work, but I have worked with clients who have had similar delusions. There is a strong genetic component to schizophrenia, however there is often one or several precipitating events that pushes a person to transition into diagnosable schizophrenia. In other words, just because a person carries the genetic risk of developing schizophrenia, it does not guarantee that they will. For the person who believes that they are John the Baptist, this belief developed at some point in their life and they cling to this idea so rigidly that it can be defined as a delusion. Often this person is constantly told by others around them "You are NOT John the Baptist!" People may tell them to snap out of it, how could they believe such a ridiculous idea? In therapy our first task is to establish a connection with the person and then to understand their world. Whether or not we believe they are John the Baptist is completely irrelevant, the person believes this and it is important to who they are. Delusions are often accompanied with intricate rules about the world and others. There is a whole way of speaking about the world, which is almost like a language unto itself. I found it so disorienting to be counseling in a second language (Chinese) while talking to people who often didn't even make sense to native speakers. But learning to work with people with psychosis is also like learning a new language. I discovered later this was a useful concept even when working with those who weren't psychotic. The therapist has to take time to learn their world, how they speak and how they think. While my role as a non-Chinese, male, intern seemed to be a huge disadvantage in the beginning it turned out to be an invaluable advantage. Many of these women had detailed and rigid worldviews, but I was a total outsider and didn't fit neatly into any of the boxes they had marked for others. Being an intern was a huge advantage too. Many of our graduate textbooks talked about completing an entire course of therapy in 12-20 sessions, but these women needed a lot more time to open up to someone and trust that person. I wasn't looking for a topic for my doctoral dissertation, but I did need to accrue a lot of clinical hours to graduate, so luckily I was in no rush.

TWELVE

Feeling Useless

My dream of becoming well-traveled, world weary and cynical came true. I was always afraid of being naïve, or having not seen enough of the world to confirm my suspicion that it was a bad place. I wanted to believe that it was a bad place, with bad people, and my time at the factory and the hospital gave me more than enough evidence to believe so. As my internship wrapped up and graduation neared, I felt all the dark things I had seen start to really weigh on me.

One of my uncles used to always say "If you have a stick, you can always find a dog to beat." I'm assuming he meant this metaphorically.[a]

Indeed if you look around, there's more than enough to be upset about. There were many hard things to accept about counseling patients at the hospital. Doing therapy for people with chronic schizophrenia is really playing the long game. It takes many hours of work for a very small amount of payoff. Some of the people I was working with would slowly release their delusional ideas, because they no longer needed them as protection. Others would begin to believe a slightly less delusional version of their delusions. But for the majority of these patients, they had been living in the hospital for many years and would likely live out the remainder of their lives in the ward. This reality forced me to confront my own twisted beliefs about what the value of a person's life really is.

Comedy is a marketplace where we are the commodity. People talk about building your brand, that is, forming yourself into a product that is marketable to a wider audience via social media, television, creative performances or likewise. You have to work your way up the ladder and earn your place in the scene. Comics are judged on their ability to deliver the goods when it comes to show time and those that can't keep up are left in the dust. It is a hypercompetitive worldview that is difficult to reconcile with long-term work in a mental health ward. Perhaps the majority of people have bought into the hypercompetitive view of life, as evidenced by the fact that there were little, if any, counseling services being provided to these chronic patients who were extremely unlikely to make a contribution to society. In fact, they were unlikely to even join mainstream society. Much of the so-called therapy I did with these people was really just being with them, listening to their stories, and respectfully reflecting back my thoughts and impressions of their life. The accomplishments that could be pointed to as a result of this therapy were very few to the outside world. I believe it mattered to the patients, but sadly some of them were so disabled that it's unlikely they would remember much of what we talked about. Some of my clients would start to improve for reasons unknown to me. Other clients seemed to get worse despite my belief that I was doing some of my best counseling. I felt quite useless.

There is a generally linear connection between effort and effectiveness as a comedian. As you grow in experience, shows get better and better. The prevailing logic of the world says why waste your time on something that you'll get nothing in return for?

During my internship I read *Compassion* by Henri Nouwen, which I believe is one of the most important books written in the past 25 years. Henri Nouwen was a successful academic working as a professor at Yale. Being a professor at one of the most prestigious universities in the world, he was at the top of one of the tallest ladders there is. At some point he decided to leave his position at Yale and go work full time at a home for adults with disabilities. His daily tasks involved helping people dress themselves in the morning or feed themselves at meal time. He records in his book the shock of going from Yale to performing menial tasks. This book *Compassion* was an outcropping of his experiences at that home. When I read this book about his experiences I was deeply inspired.

But when I really examine my feelings I know that selfishly it was a book of my own and not the experiences themselves that I wanted. He says in the book that compassion is:

"...rather than reaching down to pull people up, it is going and living among people in pain."

This place where people are hurting is like a country I want to visit, but not somewhere I want to live. Indeed I'd like to get the stamp in my passport so I can show it off to people, but if there's nothing to show for it I'd rather not go.

No, my residency is in the land of competition, not the land of compassion. I had big dreams of changing the whole system. Being a lone pioneer blazing a trail of counseling services to all those thousands of patients at the hospital that would change the system forever. First it would start small, then maybe we could do some research showing the value of investing in these people, and after that I'd be heading a huge program that would break the mold forever. The only problem was there wasn't a lot of enthusiasm for this dream. I was disappointed to see what a hopeless place the ward could be. Many of my colleagues weren't that enthusiastic about being psychiatrists. Some of them had never even wanted to go to medical school, but their families thought it would be a stable job for them. Even more frustrating was the apathy on the part of patients. How could they resign themselves to living in a hospital for the rest of their lives?

People had other priorities. Rather than overly focusing on the mundane care of patients, doctors and nurses fretted over publishing research studies in SCI journals. Sure, a SCI article wouldn't directly affect the lives of patients and their families, but might it indirectly further the cause? And at the very least a few SCI articles could further one's career and prestige. If you had to be climbing a ladder you didn't want to be on, didn't it make sense to at least climb as high as possible?

I saw that sadly we were all caught up in this dysfunctional system. We had varying levels of wanting to do our best work for the world depending on the day and time. Then at the end of it all my time at the ward came to a close. I had helped some, but not helped others. One could say that the atmosphere at the hospital was slightly better after my time there, but you could also argue that it hadn't changed at all. I was left with a nagging sense of bitterness at the unfairness of this world. My dream had come true: I was well-traveled, world weary and cynical, the mental health version of Ernest Hemmingway (though not as much of an alky).

The Placebo Effect

For someone who has spent so much time inside of church buildings I don't consider myself a church guy. To this day every time I set foot in a church I find myself a little bit on edge. Modern American churches have a language all their own, which they use to describe things. You can look up a Youtube video entitled "Things Church People Say". I find the Christian terminology confusing and sometimes just downright devoid of meaning. These words don't accurately describe the things I've seen in factories, mental hospitals and comedy clubs. Perhaps that's the appeal of comedy: it's vulgar, but there's an authenticity to that vulgarity which the church often misses.

Contradiction is the root of comedy and God's got a wicked sense of humor. I had long since left the church when I started working at the factory, because the narrative wasn't working for me. People will hold onto an illogical narrative, but they'll leave one that isn't working for them. Personal therapy for me brought to the surface my own spiritual impoverishment and left a gaping hole I was trying to fill. Ironically enough it was the academic presentation of an atheist that opened the door for me to find faith in the supernatural.

A perk of working at the hospital was sometimes visiting professors would come through and give talks that you could attend for free. One time a neuroethicist (the study of ethics in neuroscience) gave a presentation on placebo. Most people consider placebo an inactive substance because it is a mere sugar pill. In randomized control trials, when researchers are comparing the effects of a new pharmacological treatment (e.g. a newly developed antidepressant) they will divide study participants into two groups: the intervention group and control group. The control group is receiving placebo, but they don't know whether they are receiving placebo or the actual drug. This provides researchers with a baseline to consider whether this drug has effect or not. This professor was presenting data showing that placebo itself is not neutral because it changes the chemical makeup of the brain. If a doctor tells their patient directly that the medicine they're taking is a sugar pill it will not create a significant chemical change. In cases where the patient doesn't know this, there is anecdotal evidence of people receiving placebo injections for late stage cancer and going into remission. However, in these stories, when the person was told that what they had actually received was placebo the cancer came roaring back. So what is the active ingredient in sugar pills? That day the answer I walked away with was simple: faith.

Notes:

[a] It occurs to me that maybe Oreo died at the hand of my uncle and not in a blizzard.

THIRTEEN
The Narrative of "The Line"

The holy grail of comedy is to process a traumatic event through humor. A lot of my comedy is just an expression of a deep seeded anger. I have this rage problem, where something will spark me and this little switch goes off inside and the world gets blurry and it's hard to think straight. That rage started for me at age 8 when I was physically bullied and sexually abused by an older male neighbor.

For a young man to be abused at that age really breaks your mind. It happened intermittently for several years and its impact was quite deep. Still to this day a lot of my anger comes from either feeling unsafe or feeling helpless in a situation. Despite Shanghai probably being one of the safest cities on the planet, I was still afraid of being a victim of physical violence. I took on a lot of warped ideas about myself and sex at an age when I was just entering puberty. My personality changed and then changed again.

In my early childhood, I was a pretty happy kid. When the abuse started happening in 3rd and 4th grade I became more withdrawn and prone to having a temper. No one could really find the reason for the change. They took me to a psychologist who said I was probably just mourning the death of my great grandfather.

When 5th grade came around the abuse stopped but the scars remained. I buried those events deep down in my mind. I presented to my teachers and classmates as a joker who couldn't be serious. This was really the beginning of my comedy career, the time when I turned into class clown. I loved to entertain my friends or break up a serious class discussion with a sarcastic comment. Fortunately, my 5th grade teacher was very accommodating and even encouraging of my behavior. However, my 4th grade teacher, Mrs. Sheppard, would have none of it. So I wrote an illustrated biography of her life entitled *Mrs. Sheppard is Fat*, for which I received detention.

In middle school and high school, my reputation as a class clown continued to grow, but the biting rage just under the surface of my humor remained. I deeply believed myself to be a weak person who could not defend himself in a conflict, so jokes became my weapon. At that time there was no way I would physically fight a bully, but he would feel really bad about himself as a person after I finished ripping on him. I think for a long time I hid behind humor to mask my own pain and insecurity.

There's a lot of abuse and harassment stories coming out lately. As I write this, the news cycle has fresh stories everyday about the sexual misconduct and abuse perpetrated by celebrities and politicians onto their victims. As more of these stories come out it seems to fuel even stronger emotions in the arguments raging around this topic. The recent burst of stories coming out in the media about high level Hollywood and political figures has also spawned a backlash against these allegations and accusations of possible fabricated stories. Just days after it was reported that Louis C.K. had masturbated in a hotel room in front of two women he lost TV deals with both HBO and Netflix. Kevin Spacey's popular series *House of Cards* was cancelled after it was alleged he inappropriately touched a boy. Examples such as these, where accusations were followed by swift action from media companies has led some to decry that accusers have too much power and a completely unverified lie is all it takes for jealous nobodies to take down a celebrity they don't like.

The incidence of abuse and sexual harassment in America is massive. Statistics from the US Center for Disease Control show nearly 1 in 5 women have been a victim of rape![1] This survey doesn't report sexual abuse or harassment but the numbers are surely far higher than twenty percent. Unfortunately, the mainstream discussion on abuse has not caused much introspection but rather has devolved into another front on the battlefield of good guys versus bad guys.

There seems to be an arbitrary line between what constitutes exploitation and what does not. This exact standard of what's ok and not ok seems to be constantly shifting, depending on the current day or news cycle. If you think about this narrative, one message seems to be that it's okay to go right up to the line, as long as it's not crossed. There's a certain amount of hypocrisy in the current discussions on sex and power, the logic of which reminds me of the legalism of the conservative church I grew up in.

***

My earliest experiences with pornography began shortly after the abuse ceased. Addiction to pornography is not something that has been as widely studied as addiction to substances such as alcohol, tobacco or cocaine, however its use is nearly ubiquitous. My generation is the porn generation. We came of age as the technology was rapidly maturing. No longer having to go to a porn shop or buy a dirty magazine behind the counter at the local drug store, we could download it at home anytime. I remember staying at home by myself after school waiting for the dial up modem to download a digital photo of a topless woman. Of course it wasn't long before the computer provided not just photos but videos, then laptops added yet another layer to the porn experience and isolation. Now, just about any form of porn or interactive online sex experience is available and always just a google search away. Cell phones have become portable porn boxes.

To me, it seems impossible to have a complete discussion about sexual harassment and abuse without looking at the role of porn in our culture. Pornography conditions people to think sex could happen at any time in any place. This causes men to pick up on cues that are not necessarily being given by the women around them. As a teenager, college student and man in my twenties I would estimate I spent hundreds or thousands of hours consuming pornography. While the early experiences were formative, over the course of many years the twisting of one's mind and ideas can become very deep. It fills me with deep sadness to think of all the years I spent unable to have totally normal relationships with the women around me. Indeed, pornography at some point becomes a lense through which men view the world and the people in it. All porn plot lines are sex minus relationship. Even the cheesy dialogue parts of a porn movie are not real conversations but a lead-in to more sex. An actually productive dialogue about misconduct is going to have to address the objectification of women and men's desire to control them. That is going to end up indicting almost all of us.

Some people are going to take serious issue with that idea and say viewing pornography isn't the same as drugging and raping women. It's not the same as using one's immense power to exchange favors with vulnerable girls who want to get ahead in their careers. This goes back to the argument of crossing the line. Fair enough, there surely are different consequences for different actions. Few people would argue that the immediate consequences for violently raping a woman are the same as viewing pornography, but make no mistake these actions are cut from the same cloth. One is just a little further down the spectrum than the other.

The solution to the whole issue is not a matter of degree but a matter of directionality. A sustainable solution to the problem involves a restoration of healthy relationships between people and not just a Twitter takedown of those who crossed the line. The true consequences of pornography consumption are not well understood, but if one looks into the connections between the porn industry and exploiting traumatized and disadvantaged people, the links are indisputable. Moreover, it puts a wall between people and glosses over the uncomfortable realities of living in connection.

Unfortunately, in my case it was a bit of a double whammy because my primary community at that time, my church, was not open to discussing these challenges. Instead of being a group of people committed to encouraging each other to becoming the goodness we would like to see in the world, we were more of a rules based group intent on being good. I completely bought into this kind of thinking. In terms of badness (or as the church calls it 'sin'), there were levels. Some of the worst sins you could commit were things like drug use, stealing and of course sexual ones. There were also things like murder, but we just assumed the people next to us at Sunday service hadn't murdered anyone lately. This ranking of sins essentially amounted to what is called outside Christian circles as 'the line'. Stay on the right side of the line and you were good, go over the line and you ran the risk of being excluded.

We talked about repentance in church, but this term was steeped in shame. At the end of every church service our pastor would give something called The Invitation. The Invitation had two purposes: 1) if you were not a Christian and wanted to get baptized you could come forward at the end of service and confess Jesus as your Lord and Savior and be baptized. 2) If you needed to repent, you could come forward, confess your sin in front of the entire church and be forgiven. At the end of the service they would give The Invitation, sing a song, and we would all wait to see if anyone would go to the front. In my twenty plus years in this church environment, I only saw people go forward 2 or 3 times (each time it was a man). One time a guy in the audience was drunk, he went forward and gave an incoherent, rambling, 20 minute long speech about how "the devil was real" until the pastor finally wrestled the microphone away from him to everyone's relief. The only other times I saw someone go for The Invitation was because they had cheated on their wife. Usually these broken men would confess their sin through copious amounts of crying and shock from the whole congregation. Then when it was over, the pastor would pray for them.

Most of the time it was a real disaster. These guys would go sit back down and they'd be in the dog house for a while. I think I tried to keep my distance from them after their confession. Some of them would get back on the right side of the line, but I think their standing was forever diminished in the community. This didn't result in our church being porn free, or even keep men from visiting strip clubs and hiring prostitutes. It didn't foster forgiveness, it didn't restore healthy relationships between men and women. The environment just encouraged us all to bury our badness and present a life to others that wasn't crossing the line.

References:

1. https://www.cdc.gov/violenceprevention/pdf/sv-datasheet-a.pdf

2. Fralick AF, *Mrs. Sheppard is Fat* (1994) Self Published. Wolverine Lake, USA

I HUNG MY HARP
on the WILLOW
TREE

As a kid, we went to a very conservative church and Sundays were packed with religious activities. At 9am we had bible class which went into church service at 11am. Church usually let out around 1215pm and those 15 minutes were crucial if you were going out to a restaurant afterwards because the Catholics would get there before you and you had to wait for a table (I've noticed Catholics are quite punctual). Once a month we had potluck fellowship where each person in the church would cook a different dish and bring it for lunch. Those were the best Sundays. You say what you will about conservative Christians, but I will put those old church ladies' cooking up against anyone else Chinese, south-east Asian or otherwise. On the Sundays when there wasn't potluck, we would usually go home and have a delicious pot roast or venison, take a nap and do whatever (watch the Lions lose). Sunday night at 6pm we went back to the church for evening service. Evening service was basically a more boring version of the 11am service, with fewer people attending. At the front of the chapel was the pulpit from which the sermon was given and a sign hung behind the pulpit listing numbers from the current week and past week:

Attendance last Sunday 11am: 212
Attendance this Sunday 11am: 234
Collection taken last Sunday: $7,654
Collection taken this Sunday: $6,511

Attendance last Sunday 6pm: 43
Attendance this Sunday 6pm: 36

I never occurred to me that this sign was odd, but looking back it reminds me of the daily production output charts you might see on the wall of a manufacturing facility.

Sunday night service was lightly attended and my brother and I were some of the only kids to go. The services were very structured and ritualized. Prayer, Singing, Prayer, More singing, Prayer, Sermon, The Invitation, Communion, Offering, Closing Song, Closing Prayer. To be honest, I do see some value in this rigidity and predictability now, but at the time we hated the late service. Also, our church wasn't like a lot of the modern churches in the US today with stage lighting, slick videos, and a worship band where the drummer used to play backup for Alice Cooper. Our church believed that playing an instrument while worshiping God was a sin. Even tapping your foot or clapping your hands could draw a few judgemental stares. So all services were done acapella, with most of the hymns being written before 1900. It was a church rich in tradition, but we found it terribly dull. I think a lot of people at the late service felt the same way. They came out of a desire to be good and to avoid spending eternity swimming in a lava filled lake of fire whilst being poked with a pitchfork by the devil who had the voice of the lead singer for ACDC. I'm not saying it was like that for everyone, but for some there was definitely a sense of guilt which brought them back for more at 6pm.

This was in the 1990s, long before cell phones came and forever changed the way human beings experience boredom. There was more tolerance for it then and also more creative methods for dealing with tedium. If the Detroit Lions happened to be playing the late game some guys would bring a small handheld radio to church and listen through headphones. The preacher would be up front giving the sermon and these guys would be in the back few rows, crouched over. It appeared like they were in prayer or listening to the sermon intently. You knew when The Lions threw an interception or missed a field goal because a depressed sigh would come from these guys. When this happened the preacher must have thought "Wow, I'm really convicting these people today." During one particularly dull evening service the preacher said (with no irony) "…And just think, this is what heaven will be like! We'll be worshipping like this for all eternity!"

That statement came to dominate my image of heaven for many years. When I thought of the afterlife, I thought of white people in white robes singing hymns, and everything was made out of rare minerals for no apparent reason. I must confess there were no minorities or non-native English speakers in my heaven. It was a place where everyone was good and God was there, but he was kind of distant and cold. It was actually pretty lame, all the most boring people were continuing to run it like the church, minus the awesome potluck dinners because we didn't need to eat when the light of God was filling us up. For a long time I thought hell was definitely where it was all happening. That's where the musicians, artists and revolutionaries were. Jimi Hendrix and Jeff Buckley, Jack Daniels and any of the Dallas Cowboys cheerleaders who tragically passed away before their time were all there. It was a place of immense creativity and angst. Billy Joel really nailed it when he said: "I'd rather laugh with the sinners than cry with the saints."

***

Now I've come to see hell as a joyless place. A place where no light can shine. Some people say we can catch glimpses of what heaven will be like and I think that's true. Though you wouldn't know it from reading the newspapers, good things happen all the time. Family members forgive each other, communities from different ethnic backgrounds reconcile and live harmoniously, random acts of kindness occur, and people are at times surprised by undeserved graciousness from strangers. These things give us a glimpse of the world as it could be, as it should be.

When someone says to another "go to hell", I don't think one necessarily needs to wait to die before they can be in hell. I believe I've seen people who are in hell already. I've seen it in the face of family members who can't stop drinking even though it's destroying their life. I've seen it in those severely depressed patients who don't even have the energy to act on their suicidal thoughts. One time I worked with a woman who had been so badly abused that she vomited uncontrollably every ten minutes for days on end when triggered. No, unlike what they told me about "those who are going to hell" when I was a kid, these are not arrogant people who need to be taken down a notch. They need wholeness and love just like we all do.

In the same way our perception of heaven is severely distorted and gives no guidance on how we should live now. Some common views of heaven are the following: "Be good now and when you die you can live at peace" or alternatively "be good, don't engage in sensual pleasures for now, and when you die you can do all the things you refrained from in your earthly life." The problem with being good now and going to a perfect place later is that it abandons the world to its own fate. There is an overwhelming focus on personal morality, but very little consideration for the world at large. We used to sing an old hymn in my church, the opening line was "This world is not my home, I'm just a passin' through, my treasures are laid up, somewhere beyond the blue." Why would I care about global warming or economic injustice when my life here is just the waiting lounge for my long-distance flight to the afterworld?

Another flaw in mainstream concepts of heaven is that they increase the otherness of those who don't think like we do. Infidels, pagans, bigots, rebels and sinners go to hell, thereby getting what they deserve. This only increases the distance between us and our fellow people. When you combine these two concepts – (a) earth is only a temporary passage with 'real life' beginning at death and (b) hell is reserved for those who truly get what they deserve – we have the cocktail of beliefs that has enabled the Christian church to commit some of its worst atrocities and injustices, both small and major.

FIFTEEN

The Book

The word 'bible' comes the greek word 'biblia' meaning 'books'. You may remember the word biblioteca (library) from your high school Spanish class? Unfortunately the title of the book doesn't give much indication of what the book is actually about. A lot of people will say that it's a book of rules like don't do drugs, don't be gay, don't cheat on your taxes, don't murder your neighbor or steal his donkey. By contrast, consider the movie *The Shawshank Redemption*. The title kind of tells you what's going to happen: there's a prison called Shawshank and probably by the end of the movie there will be some kind of redemption. Maybe the guy escapes, maybe he finds a wormhole to another dimension, or maybe with his two friends he slowly collects clues about his wild night out in Vegas as part of a bachelor party which eventually led to his incarceration and they find his friend passed out on the roof the Bellagio hotel, but in the end they make it to their friend's wedding. Who knows?

What if instead the movie were named '*A Guy in a Prison*'? Even in this case you might have some sort of idea about what the film is about. But what if *Shawshank Redemption* was just called *The Movie*? You would have no clue what it's about and might not be that interested to see it. That's basically what the Bible has taken for its name, *The Book*. I think the reason for this is it comes from a different time when in the western world it literally was The Book. If I were the marketing guy for the bible, I might consider giving it another name so that people would have some kind of idea about the plot line. What might that name be? After reading the bible in its entirety, I think an appropriate name might be *Trying to Get Back Home*. This can basically summarize the central narrative of this book that has vastly different content, multiple authors and writing styles. Some parts read like a section from Lord of the Rings, others are poetry, still others read like a transcript from one Malcolm X's speeches – denouncing the powers of the day. But the overarching movement of the book is centered around humanity's fall and the journey back towards home.

However, the english word 'home' doesn't fully encapsulate the concept of what we are returning to. In America we talk about owning a home, going home for the holidays, or being homesick. This is typically a place or location. The Chinese word for home '*jia*' (家) does a slightly better job. In addition to being a place, home also conjures up images of community and harmony. In China, there is a much stronger concept of where one comes from and the necessity of returning to that place as a sign of respect and filial piety ('*hui lao jia*' 回老家). However, much like the old houses being torn down to make room for flashy new developments, this concept in China is also going away with each passing year.

Perhaps the Hebrew word '*shalom*' is an even better fit. Shalom is like the Shire in Lord of the Rings. A place of fullness, community, contentment, innocence, wellness and peace. A state of being, a place of rest and respite from enemies, it is also peace, freedom from war, and a joining of two opposites. The Hebrews would greet each other with shalom and also say goodbye with shalom. Shalom is when we are no longer at war with each other, with God or with ourselves. So the Bible is the story of humanity's departure from shalom and God's effort to bring us home, first through the family of a man named

Abraham, then through the nation of Israel and finally through the person of Jesus Christ.

The Hebrew word for the book of Genesis – Bereshit – literally means 'in the beginning' and those are the first words of the bible:

"In the beginning God created the heavens and the earth" – Bereshit 1:1

The opening lines are already a fairly controversial statement in our day and age. This statement includes several assumptions within it.
1. There is a God.
2. She/He/It [God] predates the universe.
3. The things around us, including us, exist as an act of intentionality.

These three assumptions alone, if taken as truth, are more than enough to dramatically change the course of a person's life. Take for example number 3 (intentionality) and apply it to a person's birth/life narrative. Consider the story of two people who grow up without their father and the difference intentionality makes in their life narrative. One grows up believing they are the result of a one night stand, a mistake. The other grows up being told that their father wanted children and looked forward to the day they'd be born. Though they both grow up as orphans, these two people will likely have wildly divergent lives.

Now let's assume that not only is number 3 (intentionality) true for this second person, but also number 1 is true. This person finds out that their father wanted to have children and shockingly their father is still alive. Parents are a life source to their children. We are irresistibly drawn to our parents and tied to them, even if we don't know them. Would this person try to find their parent? Would they want to meet them, talk to them, know more about their character? Knowing your parent provides insight into who you are.

Origin narratives and their implications

The circumstances surrounding one's conception, birth and naming have huge implications for how one will choose to live life. Take for example someone who deeply believes that their life is a mistake. Perhaps they were conceived during a one night stand, or their family abandoned them at an early age. How are they to understand the meaning of life? Perhaps their life narrative will center around a belief in their own worthlessness. This idea of one's worthlessness is extremely dangerous. For someone who believes they have no value, nothing is too terrible for them, including abusive relationships, substance abuse and suicide. Moreover, that person will behave in a way that reinforces their own worthlessness. In a sick self-fulfilling prophecy the person's actions will also convince others that they are in fact no good, a piece of trash. If 'you're a mistake' or 'you're worthless' are told to a person over and over, it gradually becomes the centerpiece of their life narrative.

Now imagine that this person somehow has a change of perspective about the events surrounding their conception and birth. They don't change any of the factual details about the event, they still were conceived during a one night stand, or indeed a family member did abandon them at a young age. However how they interpret the story changes. Instead of believing "I was a mistake" they think "I was a miracle". This thought, when it works its way down into the heart and becomes a deeply held belief will dramatically alter the outward expression of their life. They will treat every day as a gift and see grace and beauty in the world. It's as if "I was a miracle" is the trunk of a tree and other beliefs start to branch off from this one idea, ideas such as "while the world is not necessarily fair, it is essentially good". When life is not going well this person may continue to hold out hope having seen in their own existence that miracles can happen.

It's not so easy to change the central narrative of a person's life. The most commonly used form of counseling in the US is called Cognitive Behavioral Therapy (CBT). CBT says that inaccurate or unhealthy thought patterns cause a person to feel and act a certain way. Therefore, a change to healthier thinking can result in dramatic emotional and behavioral improvement. For most people this is a slow and unsteady process. If you've been told something is true your whole life, it's a tall order to throw off that narrative in favor of a new script. In CBT counseling we try to acknowledge that the old narrative is comfortable, familiar and may even feel true, but also ask whether it is leading to the kind of life the person wants to live. Take as an example the person mentioned above. Let's suppose they come to counseling for severe depression and talk with the therapist about their life narrative. Would their life be better off if they believed themselves to be a miracle rather than a mistake? Would their depressive symptoms go away? It's up to the person to decide. A counselor's job, much like that of the comic, is to pull out things of the heart and allow the client to examine them. What to keep and what to throw away is up to the client.

***

If the story behind a person's birth and conception can have such far reaching implications, how much more are the implications for a narrative of how the universe came into existence? There are many explanations for how the universe came to be, but most people do not spend significant time questioning their given creation narrative. This story is related to a person from an early age, normally by parents but also other family, friends, and teachers.

I tend towards the explanations found in the Abrahamic religions (i.e. Judaism, Christianity, and Islam) which are given in the book of Bereshit (Genesis) in the bible. I sense that for some the Genesis account may bring up different images and emotions, as it does for me as well. For a long time when I thought of Genesis – 'Creationism' as it has been termed – I thought of backwards, ignorant people. It brought to mind people who didn't believe we were having an effect on the earth's climate, those who denied evolution, or even insisted that taking medication showed a lack of faith.

However, many get caught up in the literal details of the creationist story, missing out on what is an otherwise beautiful narrative. It is a story that can bring great meaning and purpose to one's life. Bereshit was never meant to be used as a science textbook and the conversation between science and religion reaches an awkward impasse when this creation narrative is jammed into the round hole of scientific explanation.

The story begins with the intentional act of creating the world. Like lots of other great narratives, it starts with a choice between two paths, or in this case two trees.

SIXTEEN

The Story of Two Trees

I think most people have seen some kind of depiction of the garden of Eden. Usually there's an apple, a snake and some naked people. Adam and Eve are walking around the garden in these pictures and Adam conveniently happens to be standing in front of a bush that is just the right height to cover up his package. Much like how we view heaven, paradise is left up to our imaginations because only the sparsest of details are given. I think paradise was a place where all was provided for. People lived at peace with themselves, with each other and with nature. The following is a short snippet:

Bereshit chapter 2
This is the account of the creation of the heavens and the earth. When the Lord God made the earth and the heavens, neither wild plants nor grains were growing on the earth. For the Lord God had not yet sent rain to water the earth, and there were no people to cultivate the soil. Instead, springs came up from the ground and watered all the land. Then the Lord God formed the man from the dust of the ground. He breathed the breath of life into the man's nostrils, and the man became a living person.

It says that humans have the breath of life in them, this breath of life is a piece of the eternal that we carry around within us. At that time there were no people to cultivate the ground. Keep in mind that the original audience for this passage was an ancient agrarian society. Cultivating the ground was backbreaking labor, and waiting for the rains at that time probably filled them with anxiety. Too much rain or not enough rain would massively impact their livelihoods. They could even die of starvation as a result of changes in weather. So the image of springs coming up from the ground speaks of consistency, freedom from fear and safety. Cultivation of soil (i.e. farming), marked the beginning of civilization. Surplus food allowed some in society to focus on other endeavors, since they had time away from the fields. It led to specialization among different people and sectors in society.

However, this also led to the hierarchies seen in the world today. Those at the top are powerful and control those at the bottom. The top dwellers rarely work with their hands or do tasks similar to those in the field. Manual labour or menial tasks are generally reserved for those at the bottom. But if everything is already provided for, as in the garden, then there is no need to differentiate between people. The garden of Eden was therefore also a place of equality between people and between the sexes. The natural differences between men and women were used to compliment each other, not as a means to manipulate or violently dominate the other. To put it into modern terms, the Garden was a place and time free from pressures, addictions, environmental catastrophes, violence, boredom, and hatred.

The Lord God made all sorts of trees grow up from the ground—trees that were beautiful and that produced delicious fruit. In the middle of the garden he placed the tree of life and the tree of the knowledge of good and evil.
......
The Lord God placed the man in the Garden of Eden to tend and watch over it. But the Lord God warned him, "You may freely eat the fruit of every tree in the garden— except the tree of the

knowledge of good and evil. If you eat its fruit, you are sure to die."

I always wondered why God would put the opportunity for humanity's destruction right in the middle of the garden? For most of my life when I read this I thought, why would God do that? It's like putting a baby into a crib and saying "Here's a rattle for you to play with, and ugh, oh yeah, here's a chainsaw as well. Don't touch that one. " At this point in the story, the narrative can take two wildly divergent paths depending on what one chooses to believe about God's nature. If God put that temptation right in the center of the garden then maybe this life is all just one big cosmic joke. God hates us and instead of destroying us all immediately, he has chosen to troll everybody for all eternity. The narrative one chooses to believe is just that, a choice. In choosing to believe *God is cruel* one certainly wouldn't be alone and there's ample evidence on hand to support this claim.

Another way to look at this tree situation is to see it as a choice. There is something off limits in our midst, something that is not meant for us. The reasons behind why it is off limits are not clear, hence the veil of mystery surrounding this tree.

One big pitfall readers of Genesis have fallen into is pointing out the impossibility of this story. Atheists have reread and analyzed this story over and over, pointing to its gaping flaws. This story is at odds with the fossil record and with observable evidence from evolutionary studies. There's no way it can be literally true. Christians, for their part have chosen to play the fool in these discussions. Rather than taking a look at the science that's out there and trying to reconcile it with this story, we've short circuited the arguments saying that this was all by miracle. For example, dinosaurs never existed, God put bones shaped like dinosaurs in the ground to test our faith.

Let's not forget that Genesis was never meant to be a science textbook. It is a creation narrative, written to an ancient audience thousands of years before Darwin. It has been only the past hundred years that Christians have used Genesis to engage in scientific discussions, a task for which this text was never intended.

If you think of the two trees as literal trees, the fruit from one is super nutritious and the other has poisoned apples, then the story loses its central lesson. But look at the names of the two trees, the 'Tree of Life' and the 'Tree of The Knowledge of Good and Evil', and the story takes on a meaning that can still be applied to life today. We live in God's midst. Some things are meant for us and some things are meant for God. Throughout the bible this concept of God's realm (holy/sacred) and Human's realm (ordinary/profane) is shown again and again. Holy is kind of a bad word in modern english. Holy is often used to describe someone uptight, arrogant, someone who thinks they're better than you. A Holier than Thou person is somebody who makes you feel like your personal integrity can never match up with theirs. While the word holy is neutral or bad, the concept of holiness is downright offensive to 21st century sensibilities. Post-modern people have a very tough time accepting that something is off limits or unknowable. There a belief that any problem can be solved, any secret can be known and anything that can be done should be done. These concepts are essentially a description of two systems of belief, which are represented by the two trees.

So it wasn't that at the beginning of time people were living in a garden with two literal trees and one of the trees had a kind of fruit that was so nutritious it caused people to live forever, whereas another tree had apples filled with nicotine and rat poison. Rather it was that in the beginning men and women lived in harmony with nature, God, and each other. They took what was provided and it was enough. They ate from a tree called Life. Mankind hadn't embraced a philosophy of never-ending growth, which is just another name for cancer. Because they hadn't violated the boundaries between man, God, and nature, it was paradise. However, in time humans began to eat from a tree called Knowledge of Good and Evil, believing erroneously that they actually had this knowledge. They weren't able to distinguish between Good and Evil, because only God could judge. In fooling themselves, they became gods unto themselves and therefore unleashed the system we see now, which has as its main fruits violence, inequality, poverty, environmental collapse, personal pain, and war.

SEVENTEEN

Things Fall Apart

If the bible really were renamed *Trying to Get Back Home*, then by page 2 humanity is already being evicted by the landlord. They've eaten from the second tree and paradise is about to get lost. I'm aware that the following passages will be read through the lens of how we already see the universe. These read somewhat like a text message from your girlfriend at 10pm – without hearing the tone of her voice you can't tell if she's sad, happy, or pissed off.

Bereshit chapter 3
The serpent was the shrewdest of all the wild animals the Lord God had made. One day he asked the woman, "Did God really say you must not eat the fruit from any of the trees in the garden?"

"Of course we may eat fruit from the trees in the garden," the woman replied. "It's only the fruit from the tree in the middle of the garden that we are not allowed to eat. God said, 'You must not eat it or even touch it; if you do, you will die.'"

"You won't die!" the serpent replied to the woman. "God knows that your eyes will be opened as soon as you eat it, and you will be like God, knowing both good and evil." The woman was convinced. She saw that the tree was beautiful and its fruit looked delicious, and she wanted the wisdom it would give her. So she took some of the fruit and ate it. Then she gave some to her husband, who was with her, and he ate it, too. At that

moment their eyes were opened, and they suddenly felt shame at their nakedness. So they sewed fig leaves together to cover themselves.

So if this were a literal tree that would make a person die, it doesn't seem like humanity dropped dead after the first bite. I've heard some people say they think there was something in the fruit from this tree that slowly caused Adam and Eve to die. Kind of like the fruit was nicotine and flipped some genetic switch eventually causing the body to create cancer cells. I'm not even sure that it was about the fruit but more about the boundary crossing that took place. The passage says there were some immediate effects, their eyes were opened and they suddenly felt shame at their nakedness. Taking on the power of God to judge the rightness or wrongness of something, the first thing they decide is that to be naked is not good. This is the first step away from a life of trust and transparency. They began to pull back from each other and from God. For the first time, men and women put a barrier between themselves, covering their bodies with fig leaves that had been sewn together (even though the leaf of a fig tree is extremely small and not useful for covering). I wonder what specific shameful thoughts went through their minds? Did they judge themselves as ugly or unsightly? Were they ashamed for having nothing? The same shame we feel about ourselves today they felt back then.

When the cool evening breezes were blowing, the man and his wife heard the Lord God walking about in the garden. So they hid from the Lord God among the trees. Then the Lord God called to the man, "Where are you?" He replied, "I heard you walking in the garden, so I hid. I was afraid because I was naked." "Who told you that you were naked?" the Lord God

asked. *"Have you eaten from the tree whose fruit I commanded you not to eat?"* The man replied, *"It was the woman you gave me who gave me the fruit, and I ate it."* Then the Lord God asked the woman, *"What have you done?"*
"The serpent deceived me," she replied. *"That's why I ate it."*

Many people at some point in their lives ask "Where is God?" Where was God when I needed him, where was God when this tragedy happened? It's interesting that when the disconnect first happened between humanity and God, God was the first one to ask "Where are *you*?" In this scene we see for the first time the emergence of the good guy and bad guy narrative. The man blames God and the woman, the woman blames the serpent.

And then God outlines what will happen for women and men because they've chosen to eat from this tree (i.e. partake in this new system). He says to the woman:

"...And you will desire to control your husband,
   but he will rule over you."
 And to the man he said,
"Since you listened to your wife and ate from the tree
   whose fruit I commanded you not to eat,
the ground is cursed because of you.
   All your life you will struggle to scratch a living from it.
 It will grow thorns and thistles for you,
   though you will eat of its grains.
By the sweat of your brow
   will you have food to eat
until you return to the ground
   from which you were made.
For you were made from dust,
   and to dust you will return."

Thus does the curse of humankind begin to play out, the dynamics of which can still be seen in life today. Men dominate women and women manipulate men, we live in a world of broken relationships between the sexes. For men, now the ground will be cursed because of our efforts to dominate it rather than live in the system of provision that existed in the Garden. Notice it doesn't say "you are cursed because of the ground" but rather "the ground is cursed because of *you*." The cursedness of the ground continues to become more apparent year after year seeing the degradation of the environment around us.

It says that the ground "will grow thorns and thistles for you, though you will eat of its grains." Nature tends to favor diversity, but under the new system man begins to differentiate between what is useful (grain) and what is useless (thorns and thistles). The useful plants are given more room to grow at the expense of useless weeds, which are systematically wiped out. Rather than honoring diversity in nature, all things are judged by their utility to us. We become the centerpiece of nature and its destroyer.

This same twisted standard that was used on nature we also apply to relationships with others. People become grain or weeds to us. While we claim to honor and appreciate social diversity, the reality is that the human experience becomes more homogenized under the Knowledge of Good and Evil system. Those that are beautiful, sexy, artistically gifted, entertaining, or musically talented are pushed to the center of society and worshipped. These people please us with their gifts, they bring to mind our better traits, or help us unwind from our stressful day. But those who have no perceived value to us, the physically disabled, the disadvantaged, the strange foreigner, orphans, widows, older folks, and patients in the hospital, these are pushed out to the fringes of our focus.

In addition to a breaking of our relationships with each other and our relationship to work, men and women would also come to define their lives by what they did. 'By the sweat of your brow will you have food to eat'. Work would no longer be from a place of joy and confidence that we will be provided for, now it would come from a place of fear.

The Narrative of Redemptive Creativity

Sometimes I have the anxious thought "I haven't written a good joke in over [blank] months!" Looking back over years of comedy writing, it pains me to admit that all my best material was written 3 or 4 years ago. This best stuff was written over a very short period of time as well. Sometimes a new thought or experience sparks a burst of inspiration resulting in a windfall of material. I read about places like London in the 1960s or Paris in the 1920s, where clusters of artists were putting out future classics at an astonishing rate. Creative output truly does not follow a linear pattern.

I owe a lot of comedic inspiration to Jimi Hendrix. Watching old recordings of him, it's clear to see how shocked audiences were watching him live. He was doing something different, something people didn't understand, but wanted desperately to be a part of. Hendrix was way ahead of all of them, yet died at the age of 27.

27! Can you imagine doing all he did before the age of thirty? I was doing my first showcases at 27, yet he had rocketed to the top of the music world by then. But it's not the fame that really makes me jealous of Hendrix, it's his output and the depth of what he wrote. You can listen to classics like 'Hey Joe' or watch the recording of Band of Gypsies over and over again, and still catch something new in there.

I've always had a fantasy of being at the center of one of these creative bursts. Steve Martin said he had a 17 year preparation for a 3 year career. This idea of buildup and breakthrough, followed by a nearly manic level of creative productivity is a deep hope in my heart. It is an idea that I struggle not to worship.

***

Moses was a Jewish orphan, left in a basket by his mother during a time when the Pharaoh of Egypt decreed that all male children under the age of two must be eradicated. As a baby, in the midst of this genocide he was found by a woman in Pharaoh's palace and raised as a prince. As a young man, he must have known his identity as a Jew, the people who were then working as slaves in that society. Perhaps as a young man he also had a dream, similar to my dream of being a part of some crazy creative run. Maybe he had visions of being the great liberator for his people, of breaking them out of enslavement and rewriting their history.

One day he went out for a walk and saw an Egyptian beating a Jewish slave. In his desire for revenge he killed the Egyptian and buried his body in the sand. In fear of his crime being discovered he fled Egypt and went to live in the faraway land of Midian where he worked as a shepherd for forty years. During that forty year period one can only imagine what went through his mind. As he entered his late 50s and maybe even early 60s, desert life as a shepherd had become his reality. Perhaps he had resigned himself to this life. A life of bygone dreams and acceptance of reality.

As it so happens he was called out of that life. The name Moses means "drawn out". He was called both to be drawn out and to draw those around him out. God told him to go back to Egypt to free his people, but not as the young liberator he used to picture himself as, but as the stuttering middle aged man he'd become. Moses tells God "I don't speak so well, no one will listen to me" but God said, "Go and I will tell you what to say."

Through a series of events the Jews were released to leave Egypt and return to their promised land (*Trying to get Back Home*). The distance from where they were living in Egypt and the promised land was about 700 kilometers from Egypt, but it took them forty years of wandering in the desert to get there. Out in the desert they wandered in circles for years on end. This was a group of people who had been enslaved for over 400 years and though technically free they carried their slave mentality with them everywhere they went. The desert was a harsh and unforgiving environment, with none of the comforts or distractions of slave life back in Egypt. This desert period was not about punishment or giving them a standard to which they could never live up to. It was a time of teaching them the uniqueness of their calling and the deep truth of their identity.

I read this section of the Bible and think how ridiculous the things the Jews worshipped were. They bowed down to statues of cows made out of gold, worshipped poles and rocks. But if I read these stories in the context of what life was like back then, I start to see parallels in my own life. Action based in belief of a narrative is where faith takes on meaning. What do I really think is going to save me? What do I really think is going to give my life meaning? Belief in God's love is a cute idea, but often I find myself instead taking action to reach for money, for sex, or for a creative windfall that will guarantee my immortality long after I've died.

EIGHTEEN

Counter Narratives

Behind every move to control there is an inability to convince. A weak narrative must be held up by force and cannot be scrutinized, just as a weak person refuses to accept criticism. True power is expressed in humility whereas arrogance is a sign of insecurity. This is what makes the story of Jesus' life and brutal execution so unique. It is the weakest narrative you have ever heard, laughable and ridiculous. Unlike other narratives, Jesus does not come with an army, or internet censors, or a massive Twitter following. His life is the very opposite of how we view the ideal course of a career. He was a Rabbi for three years. In the first two he built a massive following, but spent year three pissing off everyone around him to the point that they killed him with the most violent means available.

His story comes with little entertainment value and few promises for success in life. He is extremely gracious, but doesn't pull any punches about who we are or the evil intentions we have. Through the story we are shown that we don't really love people like God loves us, but our openness to his love empowers us to love people in ways that we thought were impossible.

Redemptive Violence vs. Spectacle

To use the tactic of creating a spectacle in a comedy show is to draw out the dark dynamics in the room and ask them to stand under the light of scrutiny. This scrutiny is the core of auditing a narrative, it is the psychological equivalent of calling another's bluff. Comedy as an artform is one of the strongest expressions of non-violent power. You can tell a lot about a person or place by the ability they have to laugh at themselves. Engagement with humor is a sign of security and maturity. To be laughed at is to allow oneself to be criticized, realising that it will not break you.

Those espousing a weak narrative will often prop this narrative up through violence and fear. Secrecy and darkness create a fertile soil for this fear to grow in. The power of a comic rests in her or his vulnerability. One is figuratively naked on stage, judged in the moment by people in the crowd. However in this nakedness fear is being shed, and as fear is shed a comic is no longer afraid to shine the light onto the people and powers around them.

In the crucifixion, Jesus was literally naked and scrutinized before a crowd. Hecklers in that scene were shouting insults that denied his very identity. Years later Saint Paul, when speaking of Jesus' execution by the Roman government, wrote *And having disarmed the powers and authorities, he made a public spectacle of them, triumphing over them by the cross. (book of Colossians 2:15)*

Jesus came with a message of grace, but the cross was his direct attack on the system. By this act he showed us that our masters in this world do not really have our best interests in mind. Despite their effort to seem reasonable they will kill a man for drawing them out into the bright light of scrutiny.

The Line vs. Freedom

When I lived in China, I used to find a stroll through the outdoor wet market to be just as mentally refreshing as television, without the spiritual hangover from viewing so many dumb commercials. Once while looking at a fish tank in the market I had a nutty thought. These fish had been brought from the sea, put in tanks and were waiting to be picked out, chopped up and served for dinner, either that night or in a few days. But what would it take for them to return home to the ocean?

And what would it be like to be one of those fish? To be in a tiny tank, waiting around to die and be eaten. I imagined one of those fish jumping from the tank and flopping around on the pavement. This image of a flopping fish reminded me of humankind's pathetic efforts to be good people. Suppose that fish did make it out of the tank, it'd still be miles from the ocean with no way of flopping back home.

The Bible is quite thorough in its condemnation of humanity's badness. God is an artist and has immense expectations for what his creation will be, expectations that are consistently missed. On the one hand people carry around the image of a creator inside themselves, but this is overshadowed by clinging to other, lesser, false identities. Realizing true identity is freedom. Just as the fish flopping on the pavement is technically not trapped, it's not really free either. So a person can be on the right side of the Line and not be free. For that fish to really get home it would take the purchase by another, and the purposeful journey and release back into the ocean.

Release into freedom takes an outside power, it takes God among us. Commitment to this narrative is not for good people, it's not for strong people either. There have been many who have criticised organized religion as a crutch for the weak - Sigmund Freud and Jesse "the Body" Ventura just to name a few (imagine those two sitting down for a few pints together). That idea is absolutely true. Jesus once said that "the healthy don't need a doctor, the sick do". The church is at its most effective when it resembles a spiritual emergency room for the broken and dejected. And the church is at its worst when it resembles a social club for good people who have life figured out.

Forgiveness not Fairness
While the concept of grace is easy to understand, it is difficult to accept. There is a parable that Jesus told in which a landlord hires people to work in his fields during the grape harvest. According to the story the landlord goes out early in the morning and finds a bunch of people to come work in the fields. By noon, the landlord realises he's going to need more people so he goes out and hires another group of workers. In the middle of the afternoon there is still far too much work to be done, so he has to go out and hire more people yet again. Surprisingly, there is still not enough people to get all the work done and about an hour before the work day ends, the landlord goes out one final time and hires a few people who are still milling around with nothing to do. This final group of hired people are not exactly top grade guys. Unlike the first group of workers, these people slept in till lunchtime and just wasted away the afternoon having a nice time. But they caught a lucky break and just happened to be in the right place at the right time and got hired by the landlord to do a little work before the day is over.

The landlord had figured out a generous fee to pay the first group of workers. At the end of the day everybody comes into the landlord's office and he starts handing out their paychecks for the day. The guys who came first get paid and they're really happy with how much money he's given. Then the people who came around noon get paid, followed by those who came in mid-afternoon and finally the stragglers who came an hour before quitting time. Much to the chagrin of the first group, everyone else is getting paid the exact same wage as them. The payment was generous for a full days work, but for only an hour of work the payment is just ridiculous. It's wasteful, irresponsible even. The morning shift starts to complain to the landlord, but the landlord just tells them "It's my money isn't it? Can't I do what I want with my money!?"

This story is a description of God's nature. It shows his reckless generosity and our own lack of empathy. The gospel narrative is a narrative of forgiveness and grace, but not fairness. For me, my dreams came true, I lived abroad and entered into dark places. After a decade of working in these places my heart was filled with bitterness. I asked myself why did bad people continued to thrive?

But the above parable completely removes my authority to ask this question. Rather it asks "Are not the punishments and rewards in this life God's to dole out as he sees fit?" This is a very tough proposition to swallow. Imagine the people in this first group of workers, the ones who go to the fields early in the morning. These are the people in our world who eat out of biodegradable salad bowls and volunteer at soup kitchens in their free time. They genuinely want to make the world a better place. Of course making the world a better place is still worth doing. Good deeds are a calling and a reflection of our true identity. But goodness has no power to save a soul.

The latter group, those who go to work in the fields an hour before the day ends, are the modern day equivalent of deadbeat dads, corrupt politicians, and greedy uncaring stockbrokers. They left a trail of misery and chaos in their wake, but in the end decided to accept the reward God has for them. According to my understanding of this story, their reward will be no less than that of those good people.

Redemptive Creativity vs. Inherent Value

Working on the mental health ward forced me to confront my own beliefs about where value comes from. Many of the people I was working with had been institutionalized for many decades and were likely to live out the remainder of their lives in that ward. By popular society's standards these people contribute little and are a drag on those around them. I saw a lot of hopelessness and apathy from the staff at that hospital. At first this was quite shocking and upsetting, but after a while I began to notice that hopelessness in my own attitude as well. Often I would spend days counseling people at the hospital and nights at the comedy club. This contrast in environments was extremely jarring.

In comedy we tend to treat people differently depending on the quantity and quality of their creative output. Nobody cares if a comic has already written thirty minutes of inspired material, everyone is looking to that next thirty minutes. Material written last year quickly becomes stale and it's a never ending struggle to keep the output flowing. Other endeavours such as sports and business carry the same competitive mentality.

The competitiveness of society is so ingrained that even helping others becomes a competition. This could explain part of why those doctors put such serious efforts into publishing research articles. People want to have something to point to at the end of the day. In comedy, this may look like uploading a great set to YouTube or putting another credit on marketing material. Most would think only an absolute fool engages in an activity with the foreknowledge that he'll have nothing to show for it at the end of the day.

***

I don't know if this story is true, but I heard that Jerry Seinfeld keeps photos from the Hubble telescope pinned to his wall to remind himself of how small we all are. When I consider the vastness of space, my own life by comparison seems witheringly tiny. Or rather than considering space, why not consider time? Answer the following question: What were the names of your 8 great grandparents? I can only think of 2 off the top of my head. So just 3 generations from now, your own offspring probably won't even know your name, let alone what you did. And how much time do we really have left? I'm currently 34 years old, so record-breaking, best case scenario I have about seventy years ahead of me. After going through this mental exercise it's easy to lose hope. We desperately want to cling to something that will erase our nagging sense of insignificance lying just below the surface. Maybe that's why people take so many selfies, they want to leave evidence behind that they were alive.

Performing comedy in the hope of erasing one's insignificance is like inscribing your name on a toothpick and throwing it into the ocean. This is really bad news. The good news is that we carry the image of God around inside of us. Just as a son reflects the talents, inclinations and appearance of his dad, so do we reflect our father. Despite a smallness in the universe that is so small it cannot be fathomed by the human mind, we have enormous importance and love.

Everything in nature points towards diversity, but we are constantly shackled by the inclination to homogenize. Material has to be a certain way, a performance has to be a certain way, even a person has to be a certain way to be on the 'in' within the comedy realm. Standup is a powerful tool for reminding others of their precious humanity. It can heal wounds and traumas through laughter. Comedy can even bring down the powers of violence, secrecy and oppression, via narrative and emotional truth. But comedy is in no way linked to one's deep and inherent value as a person.

NINETEEN

No Longer an Orphan

Belief in the good news narrative releases burdens and pressures of life, and yet requires a complete surrender. I have for years believed in what I thought was the good news only to find out later that I was still eating from the Tree of the Knowledge of Good and Evil. I was trying to stay on the right side of the line, trying to be good. In other words, trying to save myself.

At its core, the good news narrative is about having a loving father, a lasting family and a new identity. This concept became increasingly real to me my last year in China when we went through the process of adopting a child. Adoption really rips your heart out, the highs are so high and the lows are so low. Despite its difficulty, God speaks of adoption as one of the purest ways we can understand his nature. That's why when the Bible speaks of religion it says the following:

"Pure and genuine religion in the sight of God the Father means caring for orphans and widows in their distress and refusing to let the world corrupt you."[1]

***

We were originally foster parents to our son. A bond began to form between me and my boy. Though we are biologically as far from each other as can be, I think it only took a little while for our souls to recognize one another as father and son. The love of a family began to grow amongst the three of us and we decided to adopt him.

**

Isn't the world an ironic and cruel place sometimes?

There was another fire. This time the fire wasn't in a factory and it wasn't set ablaze by a welder puffing on China's 5 cent version of Newport lights. This fire was in the home of a family somewhere in rural China who was fostering orphans and people did get hurt this time. The details of this fire I may never know, only snippets.

What I do know is that people in the governmental department that administer China's orphanages began to lose their jobs. That's because the orphanages were overburdened and they had gone out and made numerous informal arrangements for children to be in people's homes both short term and long term. This was a huge benefit to the kids, as a home is almost always better than an institution. But these arrangements were often under the table and done in good faith with trusted people in the community. This arrangement was in fact how we met our son.

We looked forward to having him in our home and continuing to bond with him throughout the arduous process of adoption. However, the bureaucrats were freaking out because several of the children in this foster home fire had been hurt. Their answer was one I've seen applied many times in China: rather than deal with something on a case by case basis, order a solution that will apply to all cases and be safer for those in charge.

So it was that foster care was canceled and our son was made to return to an orphanage six hundred miles away. We said goodbye to him two weeks after we had submitted the initial paperwork to begin the adoption process. There were no guarantees that we would be able to become his parents or even that we would see him again. We were told to bide our time, keep our heads down, our mouths shut, and not try to influence the process in any way.

God taught me a lot during those dark times. Many of us find ourselves in a similar place spiritually to where my son was after being returned to the orphanage. We have a sense that we are sons and daughters, not orphans. We have a name and a purpose, we have a family who loves us, and we desire to be loved. Still, we feel abandoned, we cry out from our hearts "My God! My God! Why have you forsaken me!? Father, why have you abandoned me?"

For our son, he was two years old at the time, and it was impossible for him to understand. He didn't know that he had a family and he didn't know that somewhere out there a father was fighting for his life and ready to welcome him home.

***

The ten months of the process passed slowly. Adoption is death by paperwork. We went from office to office, interview to interview, all the time knowing our son was sitting in an institution somewhere in central China. One of the most significant things that happened during this period was deciding to give him a new name. His orphanage had given him a name, but this was his orphan name and not his son name. We decided to name him Abner, a Hebrew name that means 'My Father is a Light'. A name is an identity and an identity is a purpose. For our son, the mention of his name is a constant reminder to him that he has a father, both heavenly and earthly. That there is someone fighting for him, someone who sees him and loves him.

At an early age we take on names, which come to define who we are. Didn't our parents tell us not to call each other names? And what terrible names we are called in the first twenty years of our life: "bitch", "loser", "fat", "stupid", "difficult", "mistake", "slut", "weak", "crazy", "ugly", etc. Given how important a name can be, is it any wonder that humanity's original task was to name things?

Bereshit 2:19-20
Now the Lord God had formed out of the ground all the wild animals and all the birds in the sky. He brought them to the man to see what he would name them; and whatever the man called each living creature, that was its name. So the man gave names to all the livestock, the birds in the sky and all the wild animals.

***

Very simply, a child knows their parent in the beginning by who feeds them. It's not about the parent's personality or comforting words in those first crucial months of life, but rather about who will sustain the life of that child.

During the first week after getting Abner out of the orphanage I looked down at him one afternoon and realized he had food still in his cheeks from breakfast. He was squirreling away food in case that meal was his last. Though a piece of paper from the government said he was our son, he didn't recognize us as his parents. He was learning to trust, and the first test was whether or not we would feed him.

Much of the bible revolves around eating. In American churches we say "give your heart to Jesus", but perhaps this is more a reflection of our own wealth and copious amounts of fried chicken. A more appropriate way to understand the journey of faith would be "give your *stomach* to Jesus". Perhaps his most controversial statement is that we should eat his flesh and drink his blood. If we take his words to be true then partaking of communion becomes an act of defiance against society's values. From the very beginning life has been a series of choices about what we will consume and what ultimately sustains us. Viewed from this perspective it is easy to understand why the Jews were made to wander in the desert for forty years. Yes, they were technically no longer slaves, but they hadn't lost that slave mentality. A slave gets his value from what he produces for his master, whereas a son or daughter is loved unconditionally by their parent. My son now has access to all that is mine. I give him my name and he can eat as much as he wants.

***

I've seen enough religion to last five lifetimes, yet much has been but a twisted version of the good news narrative. A lot of religions spend their time teaching and enforcing rules to keep adherents on the right side of the line, yet God seems to say there's something he wants to teach us when we care for the poor, the lonely, the disadvantaged. The second part of true religion is to keep from becoming corrupted. This means to live a life honoring your humanity and not believe the narratives that say you're only as good as what you produce or consume.

As I write these lines I have been a father for not even two months. Time goes by in a blur with a toddler in the house. Most days consist of eating, playing, exercising our son, and following behind him cleaning up messes. I feel that he takes my own energy and uses it for his development. When we go out he eats parts of my meal that I would otherwise eat myself, or the time I spend teaching him to walk I would otherwise spend working out at the gym. God has taught me a lot about how he relates to humanity through Abner. Having a kid in the house is chaotic. All at once you feel your adult life has been derailed. There are toys everywhere, sometimes there's food or feces spilled all over the front of your shirt or the couch. There's crying and also lots of laughter.

I am reminded of the verse that says God knows the exact number of hairs we have on our head. I used to think this was hyperbole, but now I take that statement literally. To have a child is to know another human being intimately. You know their rhythms and moods. You know the last time they've eaten, you know when they should be sleeping, you know many things about them. But the knowledge we have of our children is but a shadow of God's deep knowledge of us. We love our children as well, but with our small and imperfect love. God loves us with a depth and complexity that is beyond understanding.

To be known intimately was one of my most driving reasons for doing standup. Having an audience listen to you, especially as you relate Stage 2 and Stage 3 material is to be known. Being famous drives people in comedy as well, but what is fame other than a feeling that oneself is known and significant in the eyes of others? Likewise, sex is an intimate knowledge of another. Taken together, don't sex, fame and personal satisfaction sum up most people's draw to the stage?

My son is quickly learning about the world around him. He's learning the boundaries of his capabilities. His favorite game right now is to open and close doors. It's so bizarre, but he will sit for long stretches just opening and closing a door over and over again. He says "open!" then opens the door and closes it again. Over and over. It is the most boring game I can think of but he's absolutely fascinated by it. I am the same way sometimes. I get so caught up in one little neat trick I can do, that I fail to realize the big wide universe I'm in. Just as I hope my son one day will learn to walk on his own, read books, fall in love, experience life and joy (and not just sit in front of a door opening it over and over again), so does God hope over me that I see the fullness and complexity of life.

Notes:
[1] Book of James chapter 1 verse 27

I Hung my Harp on the Willow Tree

Throughout the history of ancient Israel, there were several times they were conquered and occupied by a foreign power. At one point they were conquered by the Babylonian King Nebuchadnezzar and brought into exile in what is now modern day Iraq. There in exile they served as slaves, artists and even administrators. Many of the beautiful Psalms and the best parts of the Bible were written during this period of exile. The book of Jeremiah reads like a modern day list of the injustices seen in America and around the world. Many sections talk about how the disadvantaged, the elderly, widows, orphans, and aliens have been forgotten and trampled upon. It strongly condemns the rampant greed and needless rush to solve problems with bloodshed. Israel was to be a light to the world and in this period there is much reflection on whether they'll ever get home and fulfill their destiny. These passages are packed with anger and nostalgia.

There is only one time in the whole Bible that willow trees are mentioned and it is in the 137th Psalm:

Beside the rivers of Babylon, we sat and wept
*   as we thought of Jerusalem.*
We put away our harps,
*   hanging them on the branches of willow trees.*
For our captors demanded a song from us.
*   Our tormentors insisted on a joyful hymn:*

"Sing us one of those songs of Jerusalem!"
But how can we sing the songs of the Lord
while in a pagan land?
If I forget you, O Jerusalem,
let my right hand forget how to play the harp.
May my tongue stick to the roof of my mouth
if I fail to remember you,
if I don't make Jerusalem my greatest joy.

Here is an entertainer living in a foreign land. He is asked to play a song to make people happy, but how can he play a happy song when all is not right in the world? The author of this psalm longs for Jerusalem, but this is not mere nostalgia. At that time Jerusalem was not a great place compared to the awesomeness of Babylon, Jerusalem being a burned out and conquered city on the fringes of empire. No, it was more than just a place, it was a chance to continue with the story of humanity's redemption. It was the longing and opportunity to fulfill destiny. In this psalm I think he realizes that his song is a gift to be shared with all. For the entertainer it would be better to forget how to play and not be able to sing, than to not use this gift for pushing the redemptive narrative forward.

Acknowledgements

Many thanks to Anas and the wait staff at 1001 Nights Restaurant, where the majority of this book was written. To Lisa Soderlund, Zhu Zhi Chao, and Dave Hicks who all gave helpful feedback on the manuscript. Thanks to Allan Theobald and Alex Przybyla who were fellow travelers during the opening stages to writing a book. I am grateful to Grayson Stallings for his calm encouragement when I was full of doubt and to Michael Wee for getting behind this project in a very practical way. Finally, it's super hacky to thank your spouse at the end of a book, but to Laurie – who wrote more than half of my jokes and whom I share a heart with – all the love and thanks aren't sufficient.

68987391R00093

Made in the USA
Columbia, SC
12 August 2019